Ingersoll Ontario Book 1 in Colour Photos, Saving Our History One Photo at a Time

Photography by Barbara Raué
©2019

Series Name: Cruising Ontario

Book 238: Ingersoll Book 1

Cover photo: 244 Oxford Street, Page 15

©All the photos in this book have been taken with my cameras. I own the rights to them. The book includes the following streets: Oxford, Thames South, Charles West and Albert.

Series Name: Cruising Ontario, Saving Our History One Photo at a Time in colour photos

Books Available in Alphabetical Order:
Aberfoyle, Acton, Ajax, Alton, Amherstburg, Ancaster, Arthur, Auburn, Aylmer, Ayr, Beaver Valley, Belfountain, Belgrave, Belleville, Bloomingdale, Blyth, Brantford, Brockville, Burford, Burlington, Caledon, Caledonia, Cambridge, Carlow, Cayuga, Chatsworth, Cheltenham, Clifford, Colborne, Collingwood, Conestogo, Delhi, Dorchester to Aylmer, Drayton, Drumbo, Dundas, Dunlop, Dunnville, Eden Mills, Elmira, Elora, Embro, Erin, Essex, Fergus, Fort Erie, Georgetown, Goderich, Grimsby, Guelph, Hagersville, Haldimand County, Hamilton, Hanover, Harriston, Hespeler, Ingersoll, Inglewood, Innerkip, Jarvis, Kingston, Kingsville, Kitchener, Lake Superior, Lincoln, Linwood, Listowel, London, Lucknow, Merrickville, Mono, Mount Brydges, Mount Forest, Mount Pleasant, Neustadt, New Hamburg, Newboro, Newport, Niagara-on-the-Lake, Niagara Falls, North Bay, Oakville, Onondaga, Orangeville, Orillia, Oshawa, Otterville, Owen Sound, Palmerston, Paris, Parry Sound, Pelham, Perth, Peterborough, Petrolia, Pickering, Port Colborne, Port Elgin, Port Hope, Port Perry, Portland, Preston, Rockwood, Sarnia, Sault Ste. Marie, Seaforth, Sheffield, Shelburne, Simcoe, Smiths Falls, Smithville, Southampton, St. Catharines, St. George, St. Jacobs, St. Marys, St. Thomas, Stoney Creek, Stouffville, Stratford, Strathroy, Sudbury, Tavistock, Terra Cotta, Thamesford, Thunder Bay, Tillsonburg, Toronto, Uxbridge, Waterdown, Waterford, Waterloo, Welland, Wellesley, West Flamborough, Westport, Whitby, Windsor, Wingham, Woodstock, York

Book 236: Strathroy
Book 237: East Zorra
Book 238-239: Ingersoll

The town of Ingersoll is ten miles from Woodstock, twenty-one miles from London, and ninety-eight from Toronto. Ingersoll was incorporated in 1865, and by the enterprise of its inhabitants enjoyed a steady and progressive growth. Most of the town was built on the sides and summit of the high gravelly banks of the River Thames, which flows through it and supplies constant water power, of which due advantage was taken by several factories at the waterside. The town got its name from a pioneer family named Ingersoll, who were among the first settlers in this district and took a very prominent part in the early career of the community.

It was situated on the Great Western Division of the Grand Trunk Railway, and also on the Credit Valley Branch of the Canadian Pacific. The country around is fertile, and large quantities of cheese were shipped from here. The manufacture of flour and cornmeal, with woolen and planing mills, a tannery and four agricultural implement factories, formed its chief industries; grain, livestock, and general manufactured products, in addition to cheese, formed its chief shipments.

In 1886 a special effort was made to induce desirable factories to locate here and in the following year the John Morrow Machine Screw Works, the Evans Bros. and Littler Piano factory and the Hault furniture factory were secured by giving liberal bonuses. Later on, the St. Charles Condenser and the Ingersoll Nut Factory were opened.

Ingersoll was the first town in Canada to adopt the silica-barytic sidewalks in 1890 when a contract was given to Otto Guelich of Detroit, to construct a sidewalk on the east side of Thames Street from the Atlantic House to the Baptist Tabernacle, a distance of three blocks. In 1891 a local company was organized with Walter Mills as manager, and year by year the work has been carried on till now nearly every street on both sides has a nice, clean, smooth silica-barytic sidewalk, totaling about fifty miles.

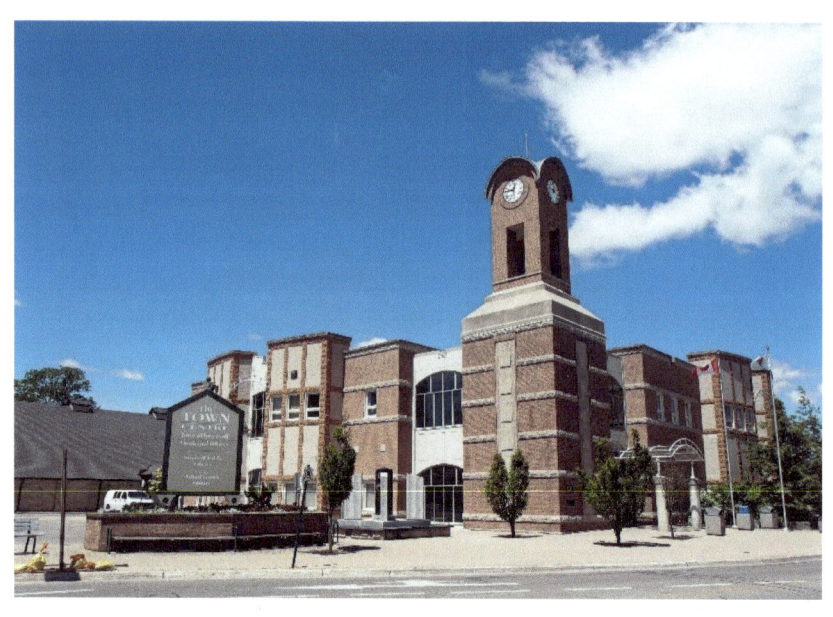

130 Oxford Street – Ingersoll Town Centre

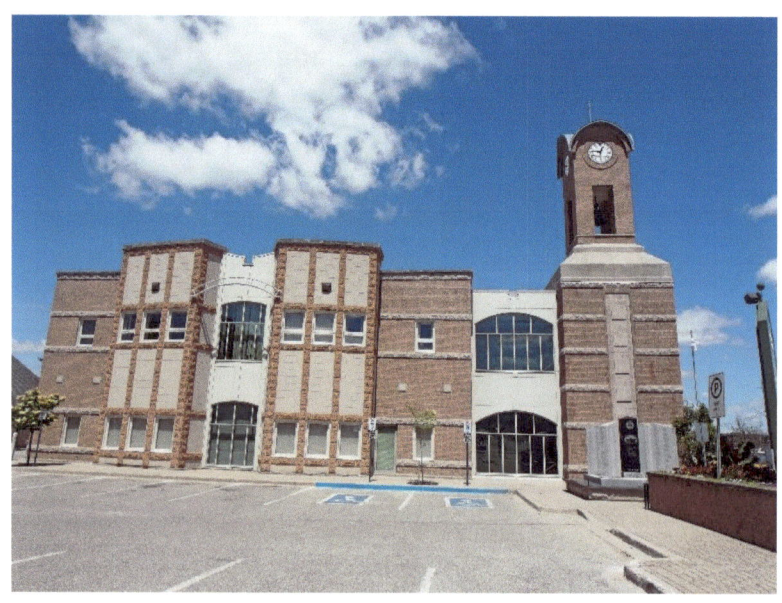

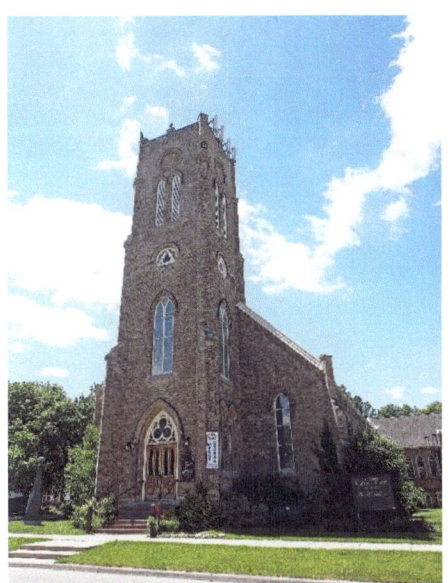 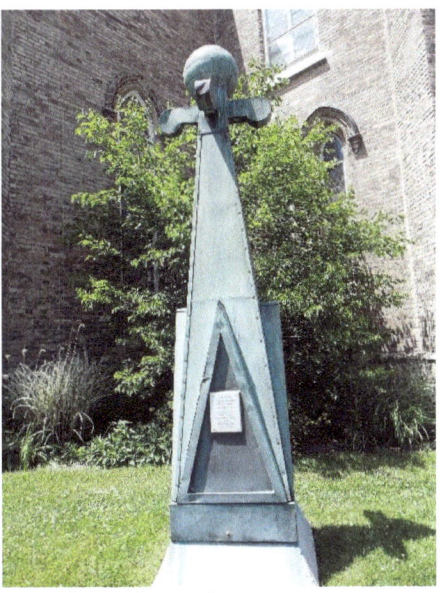

Oxford Street – St. James Anglican Church – There were originally four of these pinnacles on the top of the church. Gothic Revival – lancet windows with muntins, trefoil above door, four-storey tower

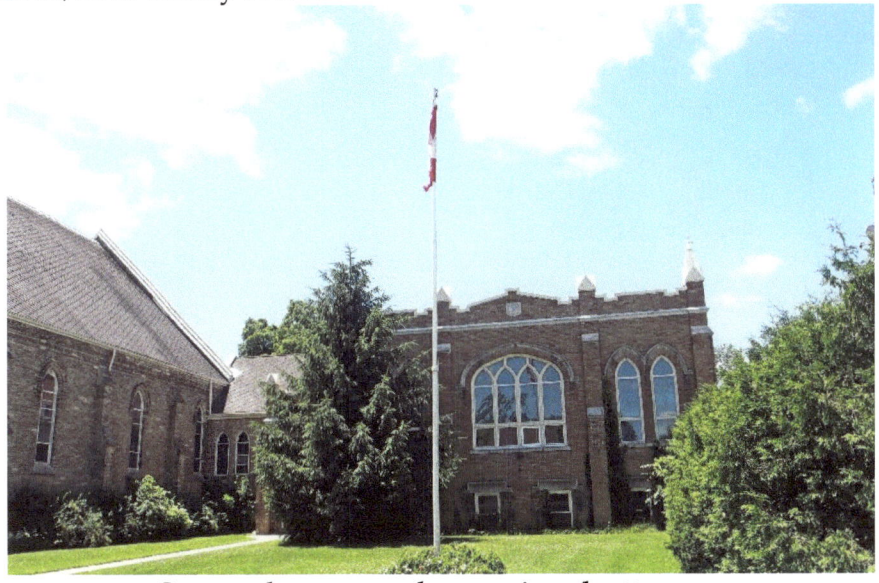

Stepped parapet above wing, buttresses

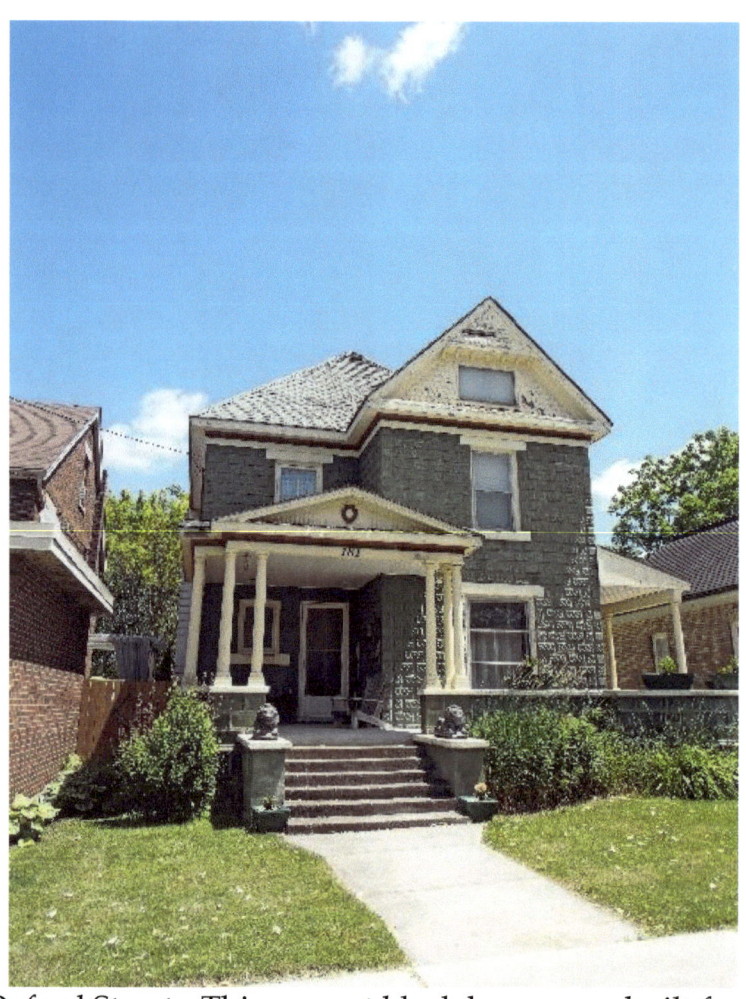

181 Oxford Street - This cement block house was built for R.A. Skinner who owned and operated Skinner's Livery on the north side of Charles Street at the Oxford corner. Stained-glass panel on first floor window; pediment above porch with Doric pillars; a lion on either side of the front steps. This home was the scene of many elaborate house parties, the form of entertainment that made up the fabric of social life of the times. The Skinner Livery, sometimes referred to as the Bon Ton Livery, maintained vehicles for pleasure driving, business trips, weddings, funerals, etc.

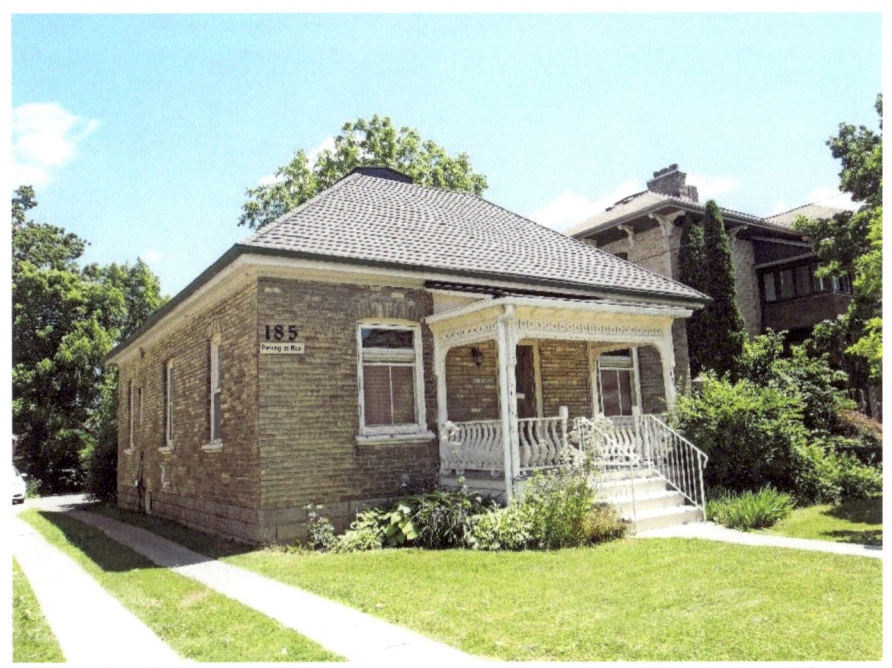

185 Oxford Street – This one-storey Regency Cottage with a hipped roof is over one hundred years old. Its most attractive features are the front porch with the decorative fascia board, molded brackets and interesting railing construction and the two stained-glass panels in the front windows. This house was built for his sister by F. Richardson, lumber dealer and owner of a planing mill. He became involved in the lumber business around 1885 and erected or supplied lumber for many buildings in the area.

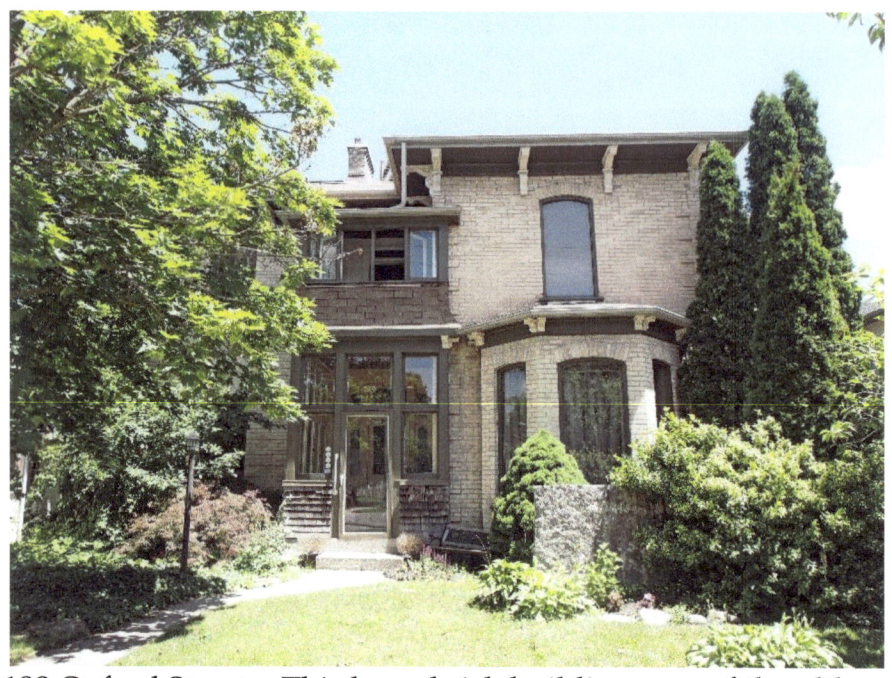

189 Oxford Street – This large brick building, one of the older homes in this section of Oxford Street, was erected by the Christopher Brothers and occupied by Aaron Christopher for a number of years. The broad bracketed eave of the Italianate style was common in Ontario around 1860. The Christopher Brothers were well known Ingersoll contractors who built many structures, still in use in the Town (e.g. Daly House and the Anglican Church, as well as many quality homes). It has a bay window with three windows.

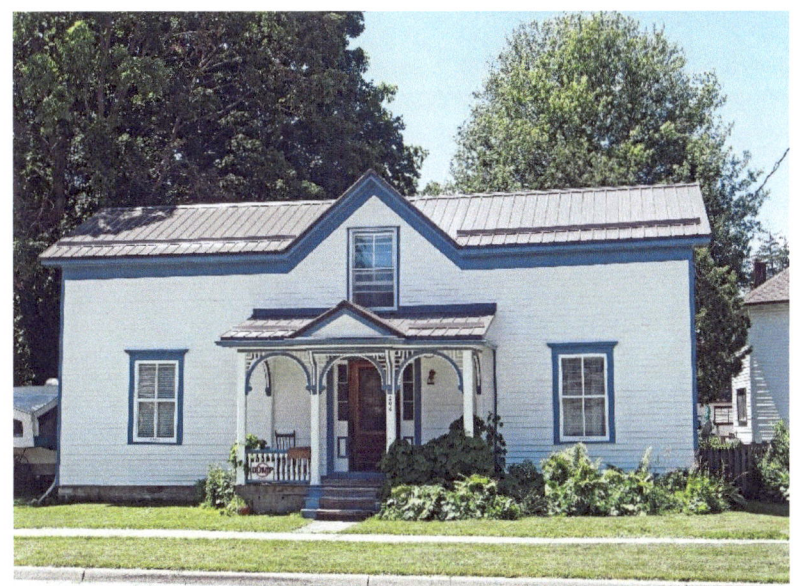

206 Oxford Street – Ontario Cottage with center gable

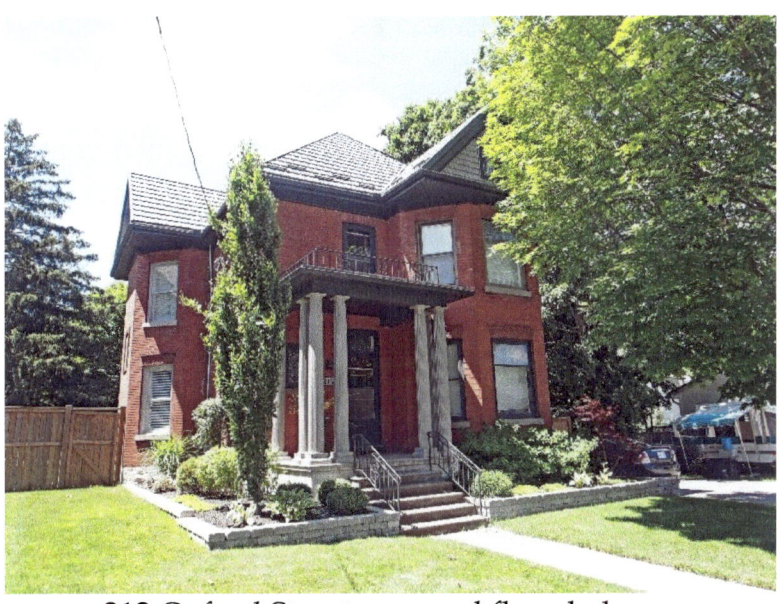

212 Oxford Street – second floor balcony

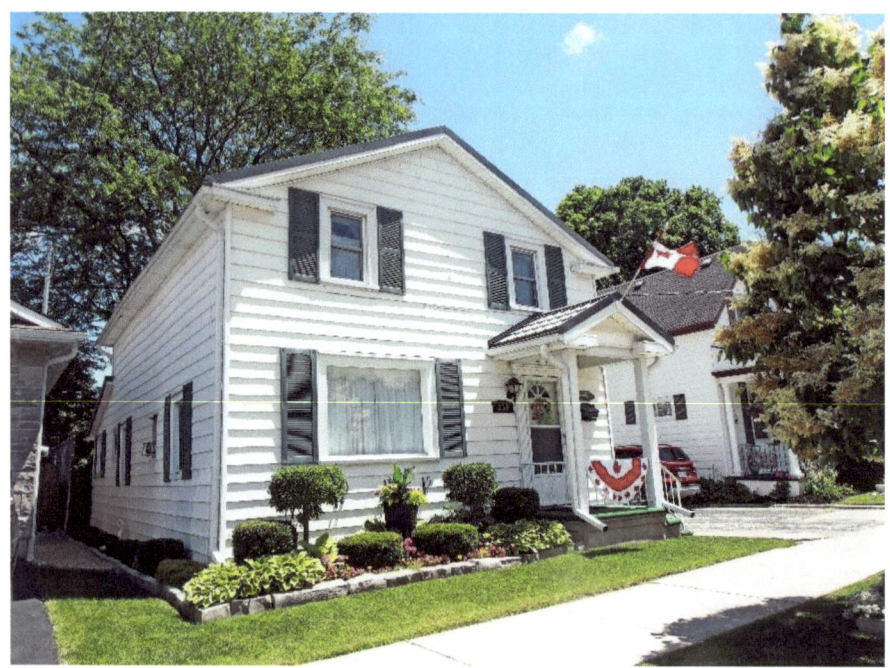

213 Oxford Street - This dwelling, commonly referred to as the Gray House, was built in three sections. The angled window frame on the south side is typical of the architectural style of the 1850s and 1860s. It was purchased by Benjamin Gray in 1895 for $450.00 from John Hugi II, well known Ingersoll Photographer. At one time Benjamin Gray was the market clerk at the Town Hall and he also collected the rental fee, sometimes as low as $1.00, for the use of the auditorium. There is a cornice return on the large gable and on the pediment above the porch which is supported by square pillars.

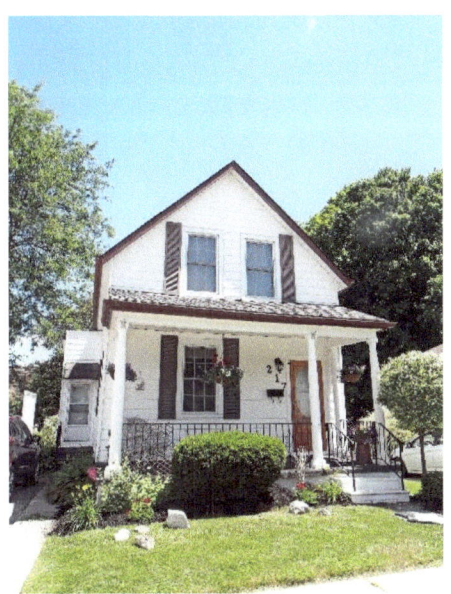

217 Oxford Street

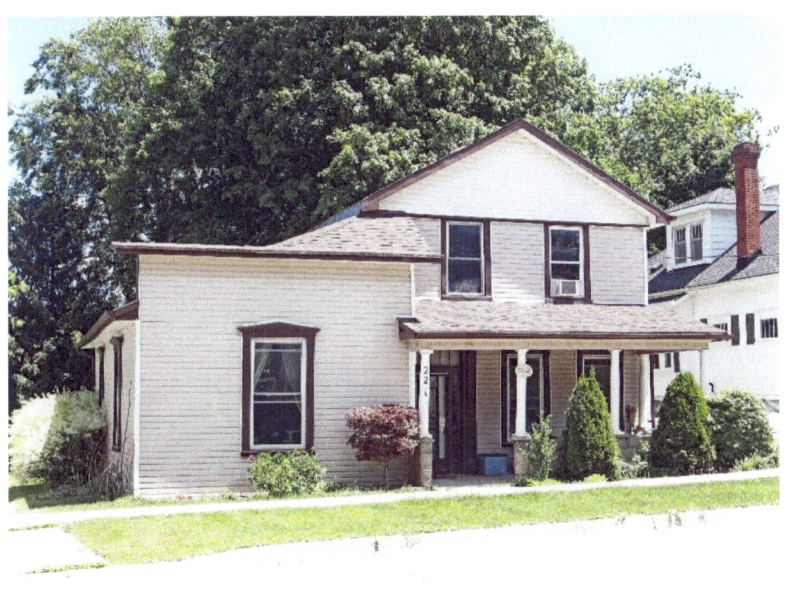

221 Oxford Street

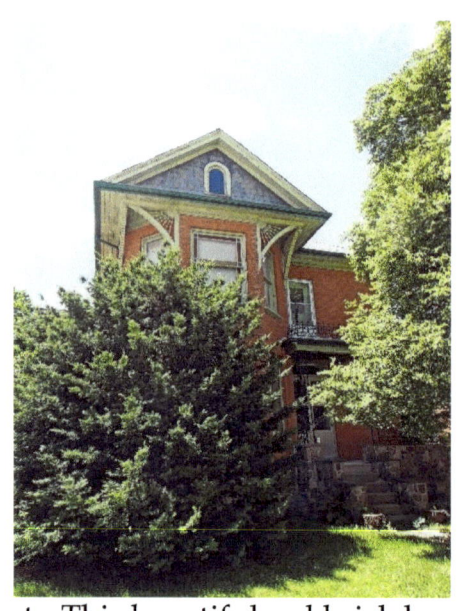

218 Oxford Street - This beautiful red brick home was built in 1896 for Henry G. Boyse. He owned and operated a farm near Verschoyle where he was born. Later he moved to Ingersoll and opened a flour and feed store at 70 Thames Street North. The roofing is the original Welsh Slate as is the iron work around the roof top and porch railing.

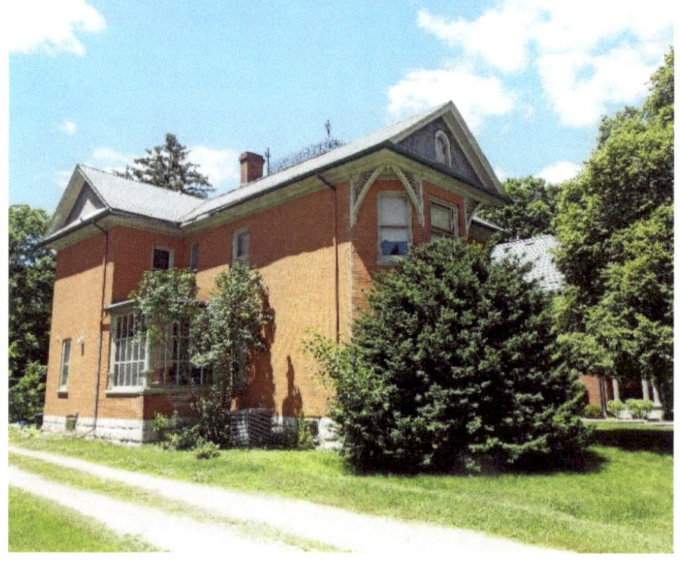

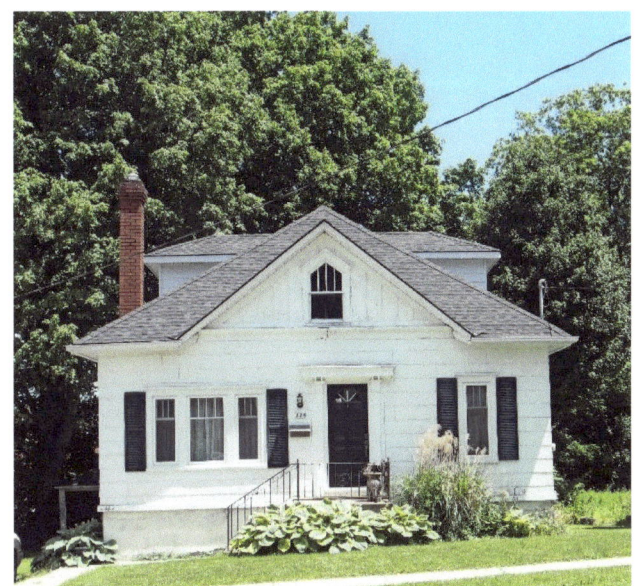

225 Oxford Street

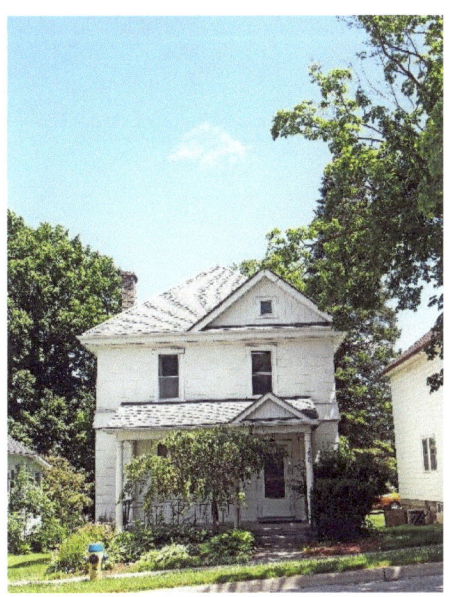

229 Oxford Street

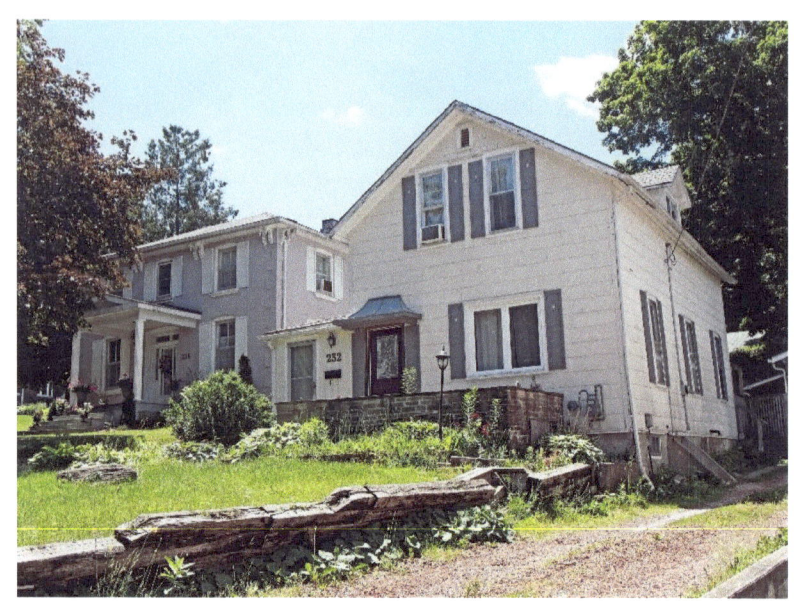

232 Oxford Street

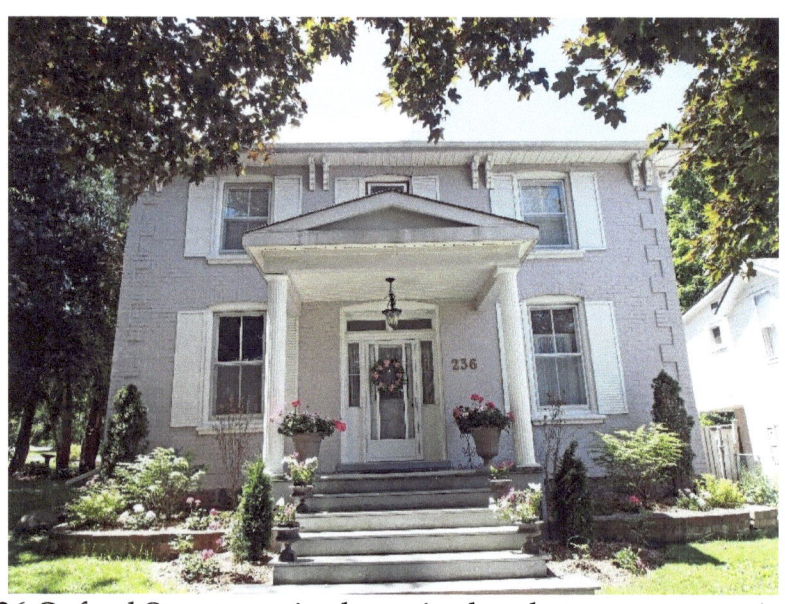

236 Oxford Street – paired cornice brackets, corner quoins, pediment above porch, sidelights and transom window

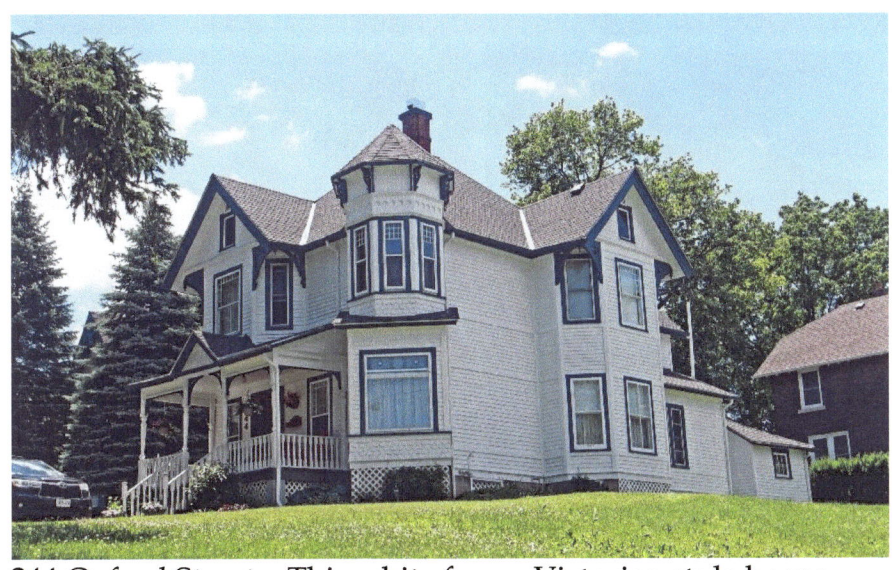

244 Oxford Street – This white frame Victorian style house was built by Justus Miller in 1895. In the 1880s he and his brother became successful contractors for the Dominion Government, constructing such large public works as canal locks, docks, etc. After moving to Mount Elgin, he became engaged in the lumber business. The mass production of thin studs and joists replaced the massive timbers needed to frame a house. These homes were termed "Stick Style". This house incorporated a whimsical tower, bay windows, interesting roof angles and a veranda with softly curved arches and fancy woodwork.

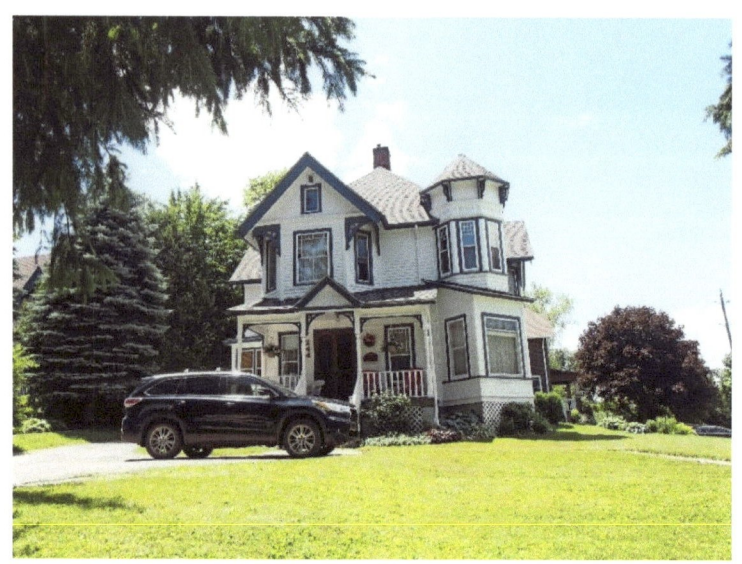

244 Oxford Street

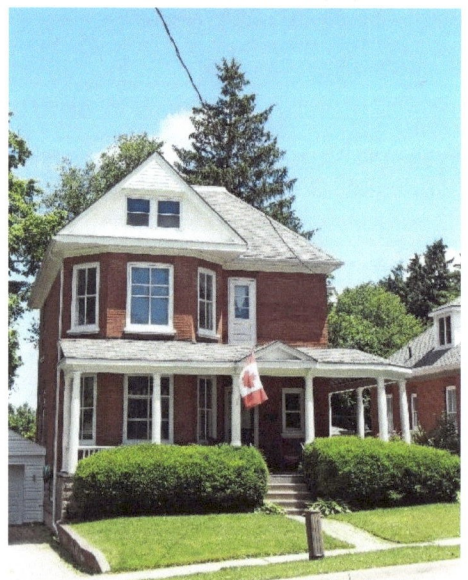

253 Oxford Street - This home, built by Foster Wilson, a prominent Ingersoll builder, is similar in style to the one at 114 Frances Street by the same contractor. Chestnut, which was becoming popular, is used extensively throughout the house.

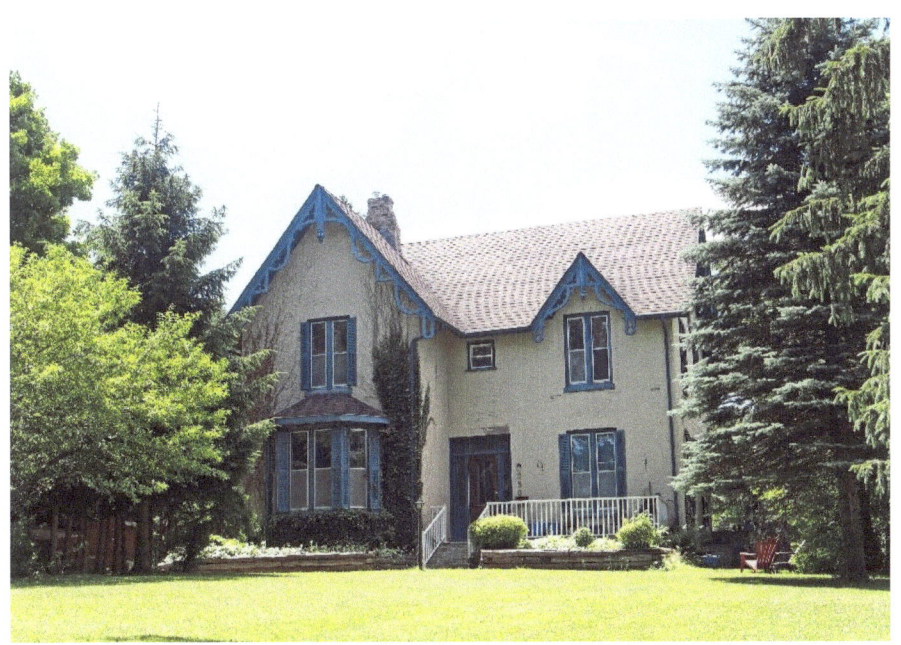

250 Oxford Street – Decorative bargeboard (gingerbread), taken from designs found in windows of medieval churches, became a popular addition to houses in the 1860s. It was cut from three-inch-thick pine boards. The earliest bargeboard was more board than space but later took on a lacy look, indicating that this dwelling was built circa 1880-1890. The gables of this Victoria home are further emphasized by the addition of the finials. The original yellow brick has been painted.

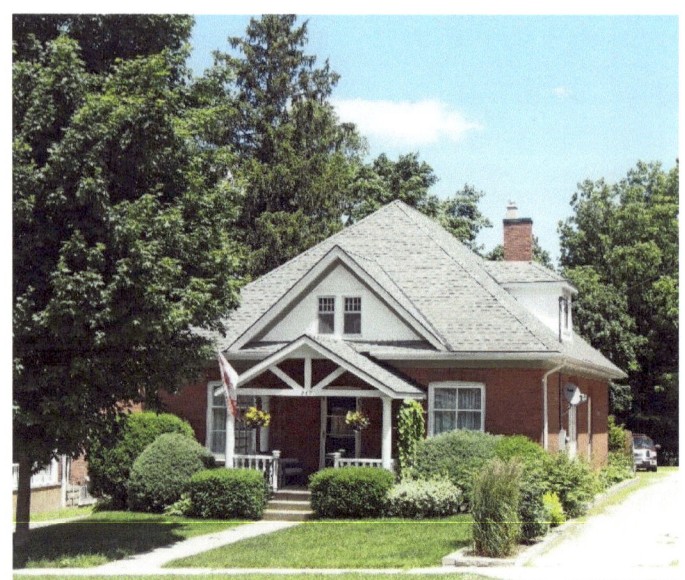

257 Oxford Street - Originally this house was a frame dwelling located in the center of a larger lot. Later it was moved a short distance to the south and bricked. Subsequently the lot was divided and the house at 253 was built.

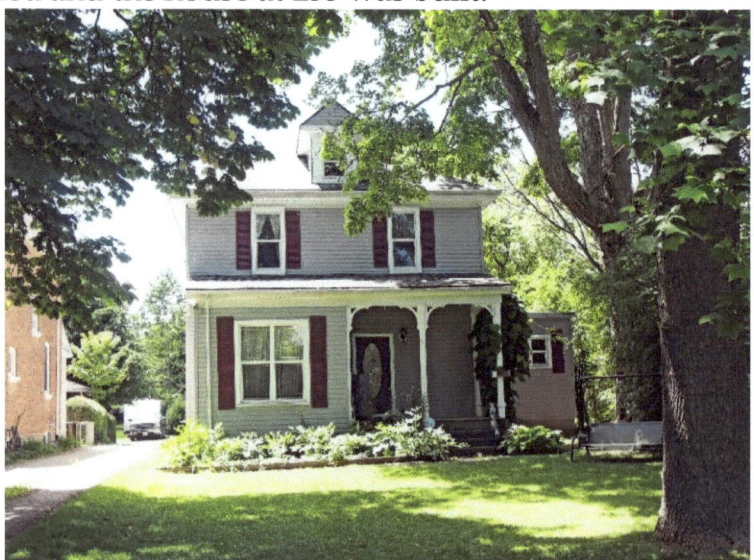

282 Oxford Street - The white stucco house was built by Justus Miller. There is a dormer in the attic.

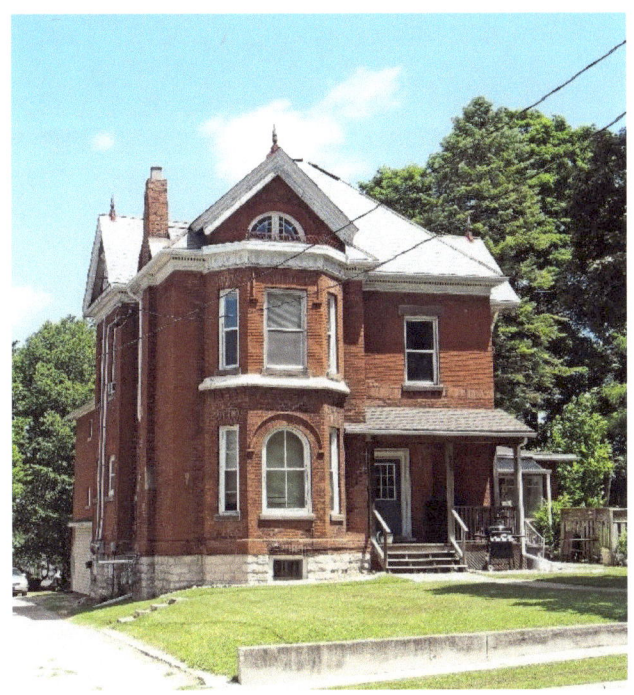

261 Oxford Street – This house built circa 1882 was one of the first to be constructed of the smooth red brick which became available at this time. The exterior walls were double bricked. Brick was also used for some of the interior wall construction which became apparent when a former owner removed two of the walls to enlarge a room. On the south side was a conservatory and green house which was replaced by a sun room. A dumb waiter, with several shelves and sliding glass doors, allowed food to be raised to the kitchen from the basement which was used as a cold storage. Originally the house had five fireplaces. Beautifully carved woodwork adorns the remaining mantles as well as the banister railing. Mr. Spencer Freeman was the original owner. Later C.W. Riley, a local cheese maker bought the property. He was the nephew of C.W. Riley Sr. "Cheese King of Western Ontario" and took over the ownership of Slawson's Cheese Company, Ingersoll from his uncle. There is a two-storey bay window; finials on gables.

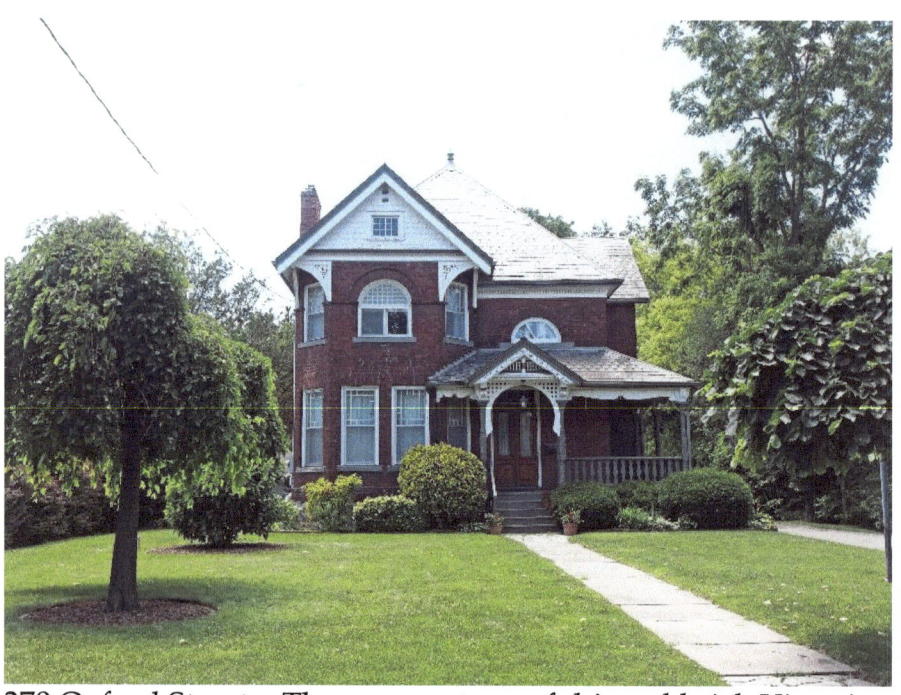

270 Oxford Street – The corner stone of this red brick Victorian home built in 1897 was discovered during renovations and bears the name "Buchanan". The property was purchased in the early 1900s by Mr. & Mrs. G. Bartlett, clothing merchants in Ingersoll for many years. The home with its eleven-foot ceilings has four bedrooms, the original "maids" staircase and an elegant winding cherry staircase in the front hall. The fretwork design paneling and the beveled glass in the front door and in upstairs windows have been preserved.

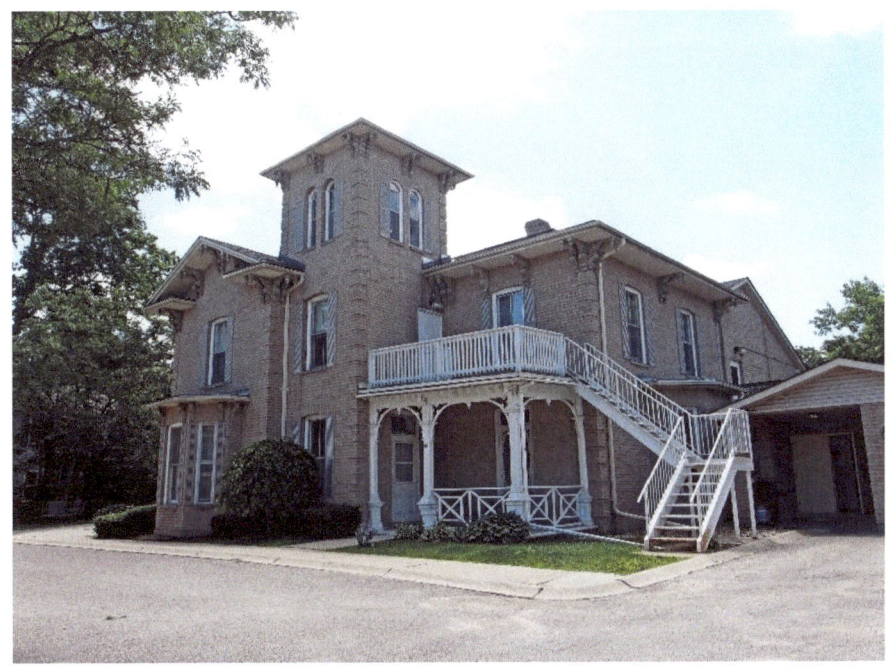

276 Oxford Street – Oxford Manor Retirement Home – This large yellow brick Italianate Villa style home was built circa 1880 by the Christopher Brothers and was the residence of Aaron Christopher. The design was introduced in England at the beginning of Queen Victoria's reign as a model suburban housing for the rising mercantile class. Its main feature is the central Tuscan Tower with its tall rounded Italianate style windows and eaves.

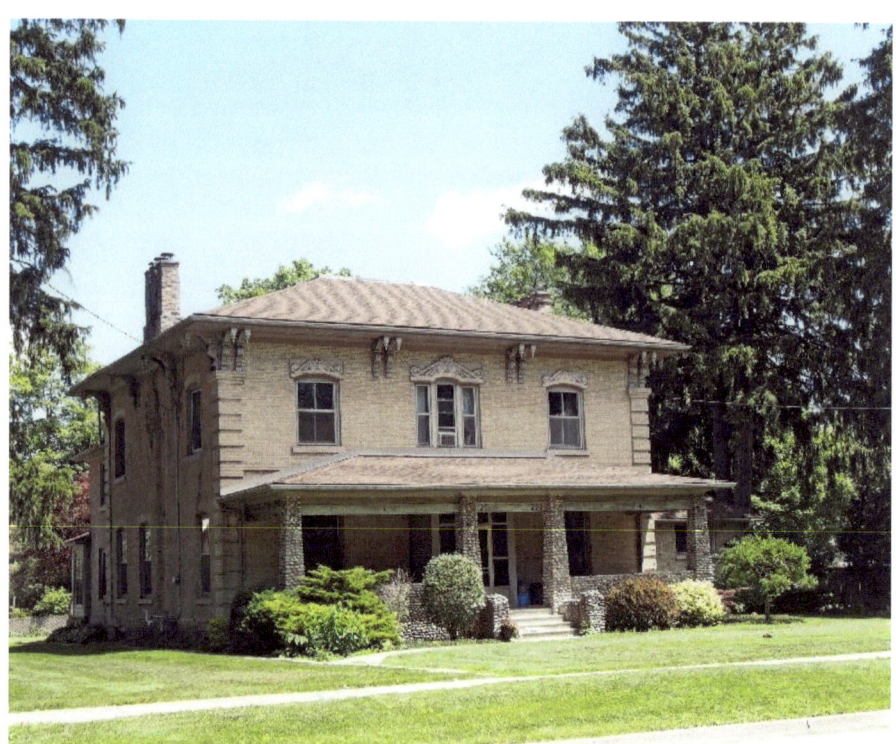

291-293 Oxford Street – This home was built around 1880 and illustrates the typical broad bracketed eaves of the Italianate style. Fred J. Stone was one of the earliest occupants of this yellow brick house. He joined Wm. Stones Sons Ltd. in 1907 as manager of the Ingersoll branch. The operation started as a hide and wool business but soon developed into a fertilizer plant, later expanding to make livestock feed concentrates. In the 1920s it passed into the possession of W.A.C. Forman, a family relative. At this time the house was divided to accommodate two units. His father owned the "FAIR", a store at 126 Thames St. South which sold dry goods and household furnishings and utensils. When the store came under the management of Mr. Forman Jr., it became known as "Forman's Set - $1.00". It has a hipped roof, paired cornice brackets, and corner quoins.

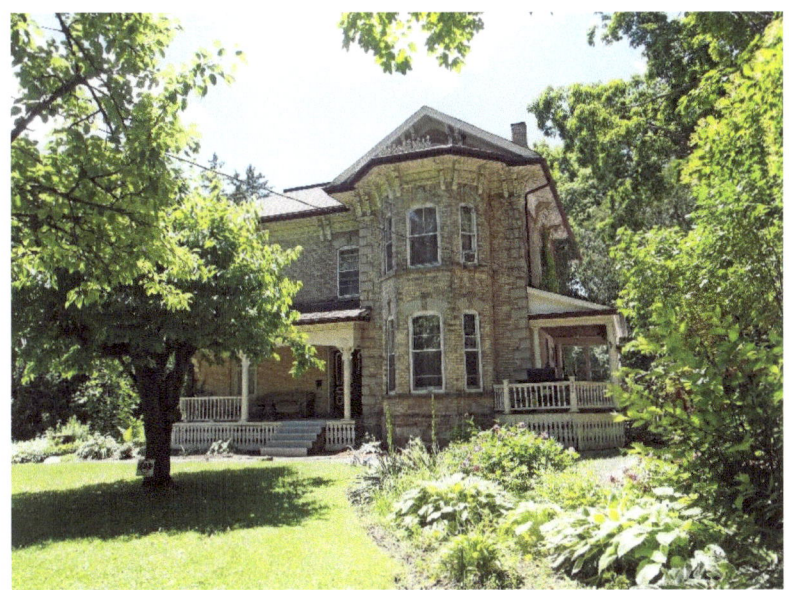

296 Oxford Street – 2½-storey bay with cornice brackets

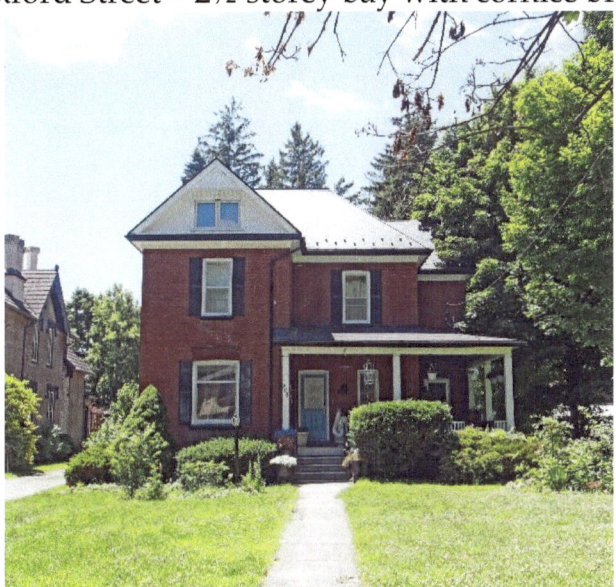

304 Oxford Street - This red brick house was built in 1903 for James Kerr, a partner in the business of Smith and Kerr, men's clothing store, on Thames Street. George Smith opened the store in Ingersoll in the late 1870s; Mr. Kerr joined 1907.

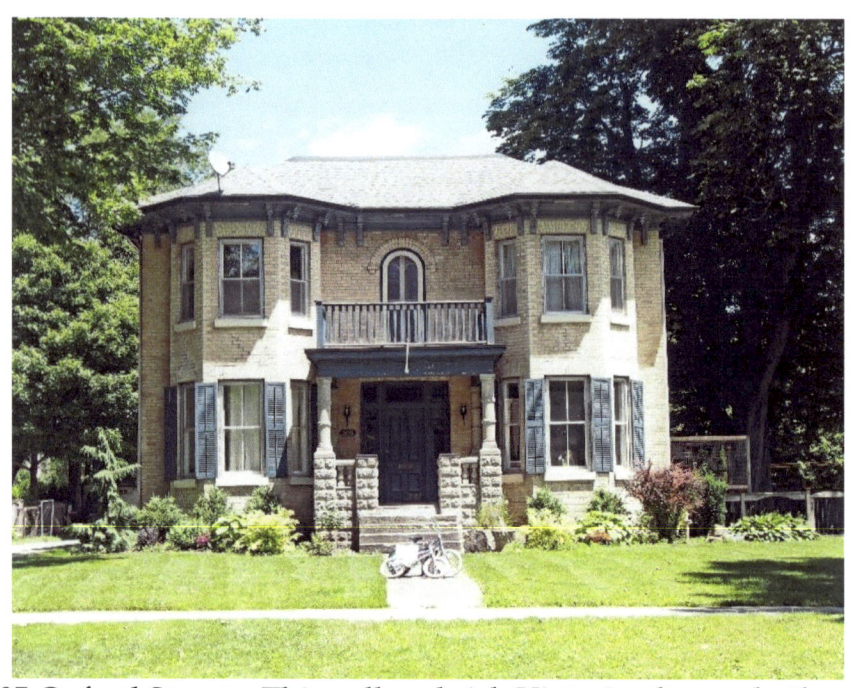

305 Oxford Street – This yellow brick Victorian home, built circa 1865, features a two-storey detached barn where the original occupants stabled their horses and carriages. Mr. Richard Seldon and his daughter, Annie, who lived here from 1894 to 1967, served as Clerks for the Township of North Oxford. Between 1918 and 1967 residents came to the house to pay their taxes in what is now the formal dining room. High ceilings, elaborate moldings, wide baseboards and pine floors grace each of the formal rooms in the main part of the house. The brass chandeliers in the dining room and lower hall are original, as is the fireplace in the parlor. Molded cherubs decorate one of the two curved archways upstairs. The servants' quarters were located in the rear portion of the house along with the summer kitchen which retains its original painted tin ceiling. The Seldon House with its triple brick exterior walls was built to last. It has paired cornice brackets, a second-floor balcony, and two-storey bay windows.

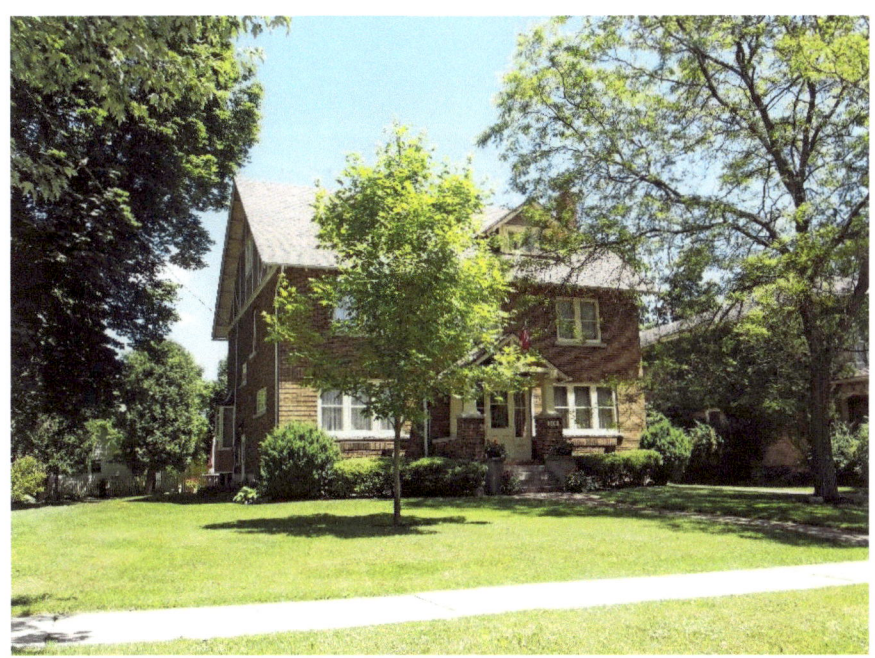

309 Oxford Street - The original house was built circa 1877. John Turner and Harley Copeland were two of the former owners. It was the St. James Anglican Manse for a number of years before being destroyed by fire. In 1928 Jack Eidt rebuilt the present house. The rafters and the stain glass window in the rear sunroom came from the Ebenezer Church located one mile north of VerschoyIe. The removable oak panels protecting the front entrance during the winter were originally the front doors of the same church. The hand cut stone window sills were made by Pounder Plumbing & Planing Mill, Stratford, using stone from the St. Mary's Quarry. Many of the beveled glass windows are further highlighted with a cut glass cornflower design. On the wall above the mantle, is a mural of an old English castle scene which was created by a Dutch painter using paint tinted with marble dust to help preserve the rich colors. The upper part of the garage at the rear of the property was used as a chicken and brooder house in connection with his feed business located at 70 Thames Street North.

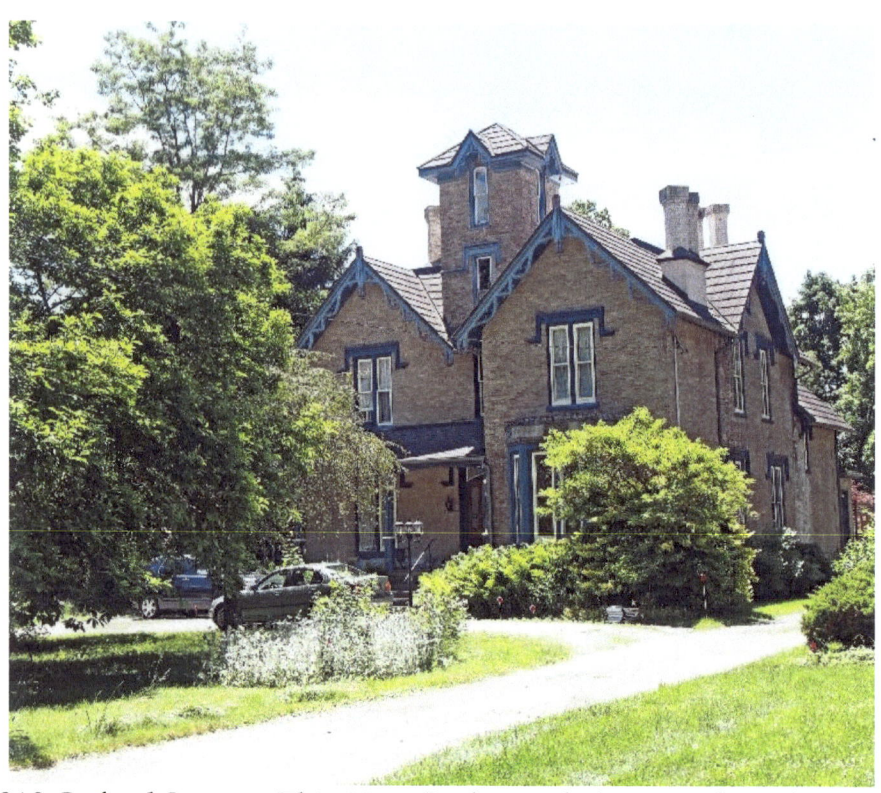

310 Oxford Street – This Neo-Gothic style home referred to as the "Gayfer House" was built in 1863 by Noxon. Except for the removal of a wrought iron fence bordering the street, the house from the front appears as it did when first built. In the early 1900s the rear wing was demolished and a sun room, pantry and rear vestibule were erected using the original brick. The three chimneys are chimney flues and ventilation chimneys. The original roofing was slate. Guy Lumbardo played in this house for the "Coming Out" party of Dorothy Gayfer with over two hundred invited guests. According to a granddaughter of John Gayfer, the tower was used for learning to smoke! The land and premises were purchased by Louise and John Gayfer (a well-known Ingersoll druggist) in 1881 and remained in the Gayfer family until the 1960s.

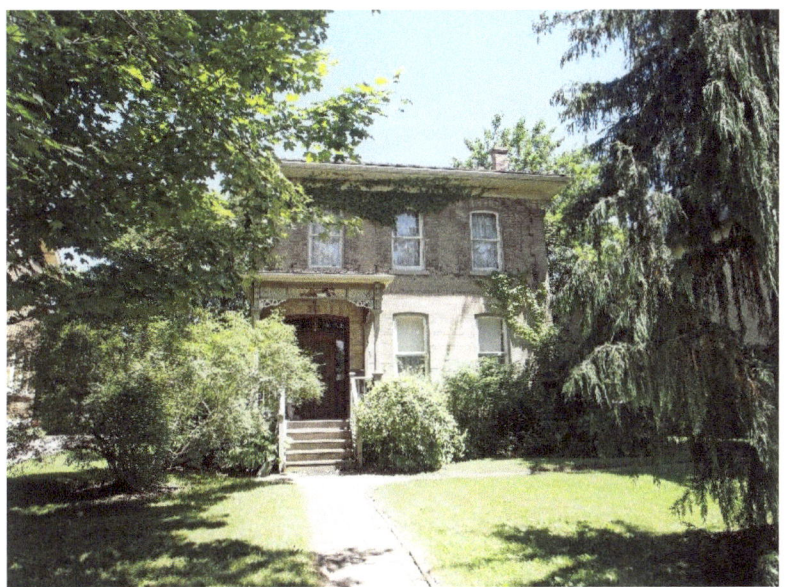

315 Oxford Street – hipped roof - This brick house was once owned by John Banbury, former Minister of Agriculture.

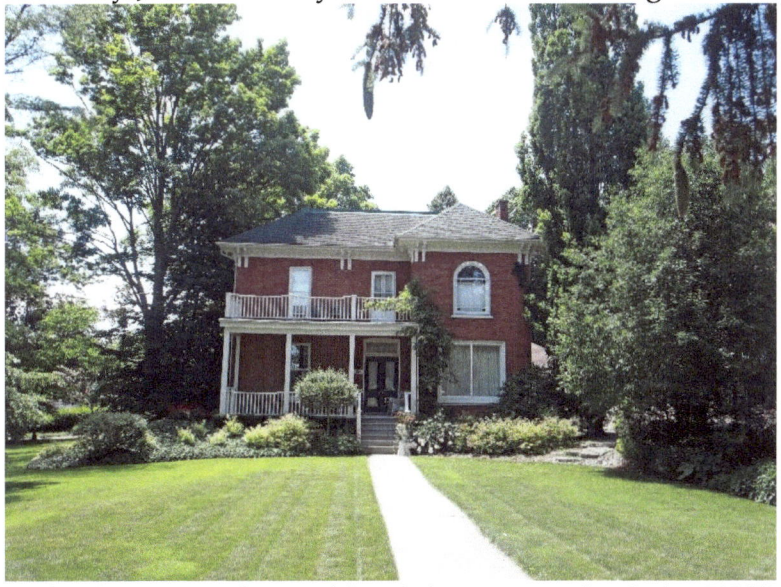

320 Oxford Street - This red brick house was built for William Thompson circa 1890. Later he added the section at the rear enlarging the house to accommodate six bedrooms.

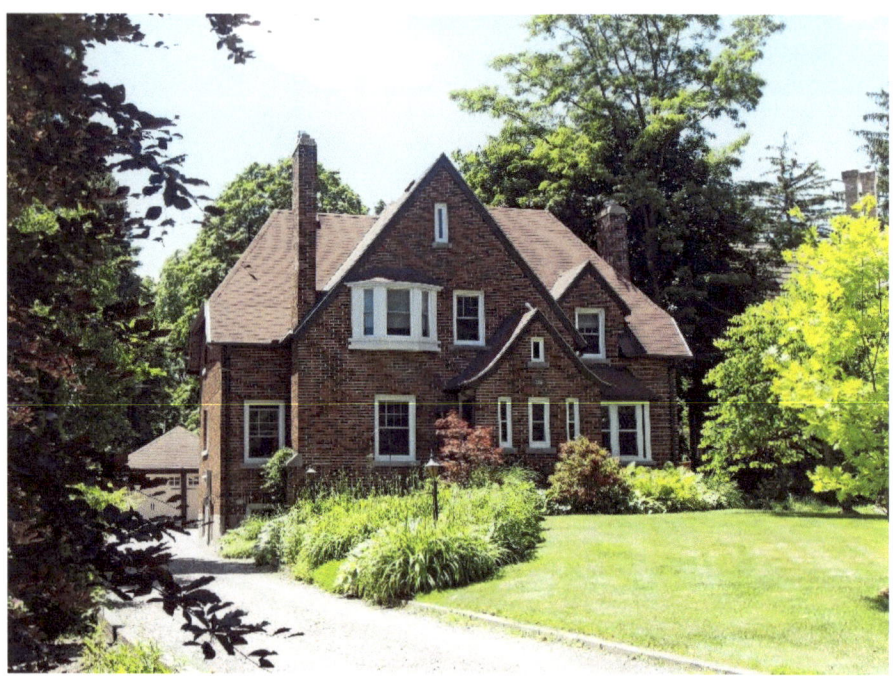

316 Oxford Street - Many of the features of a Tudor style house have been incorporated in this home, including the patterned brick work, interesting chimney treatment, groups of rectangular windows, and complex roof line with many gables. Straight clean lines and design are typical. The home was built in 1937 and given to Harold and Lorna Wilson by his father E.A. Wilson as a wedding present. The Wilson family owned the Ingersoll Machine & Tool Company and were also involved in speed boat racing. In 1939 Harold won the President's Cup with his craft "Miss Canada", making the first time in U.S. boat racing history that the cup was won by a foreigner. Harold is included in the Canada's Sports Hall of Fame.

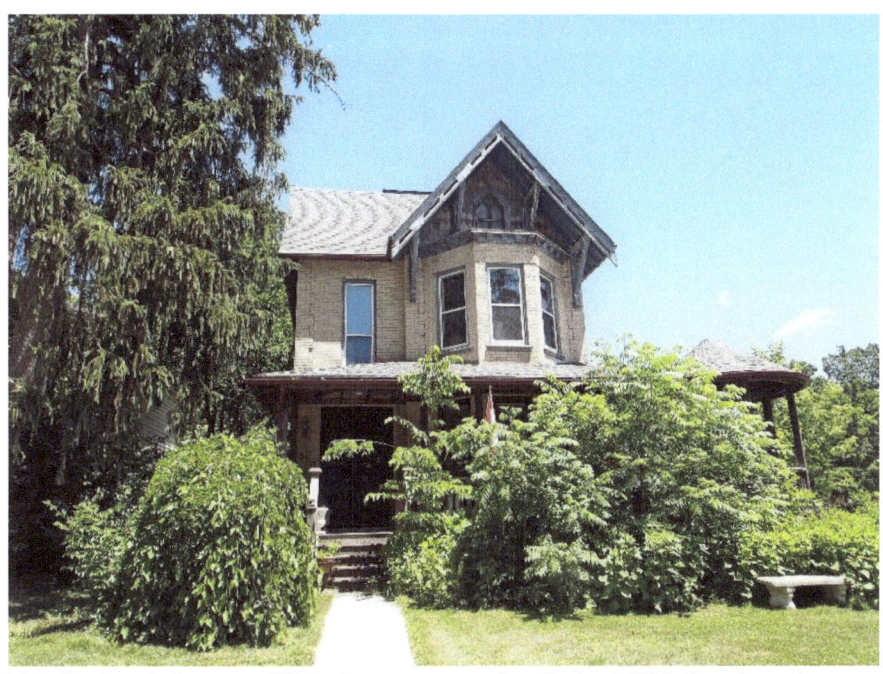

319 Oxford Street - This house was built in 1888 for Stephen Noxon, treasurer of Noxon Brothers Agricultural Works. The company started in 1856. Noxon supported the hospital project, naming a ward in Alexandra Hospital after his wife Jessie as well as furnishing a ward in memory of his daughter, Louise, who died very young. Originally this home had front and side verandas and at the rear was an archway to accommodate a horse and carriage. The extended gable at the front protects the bay window section from inclement weather. Soldiers returning from World War I duty were entertained in the large living room. A dance floor was improvised by stretching linen tightly over the rug and fastening it securely along the walls.

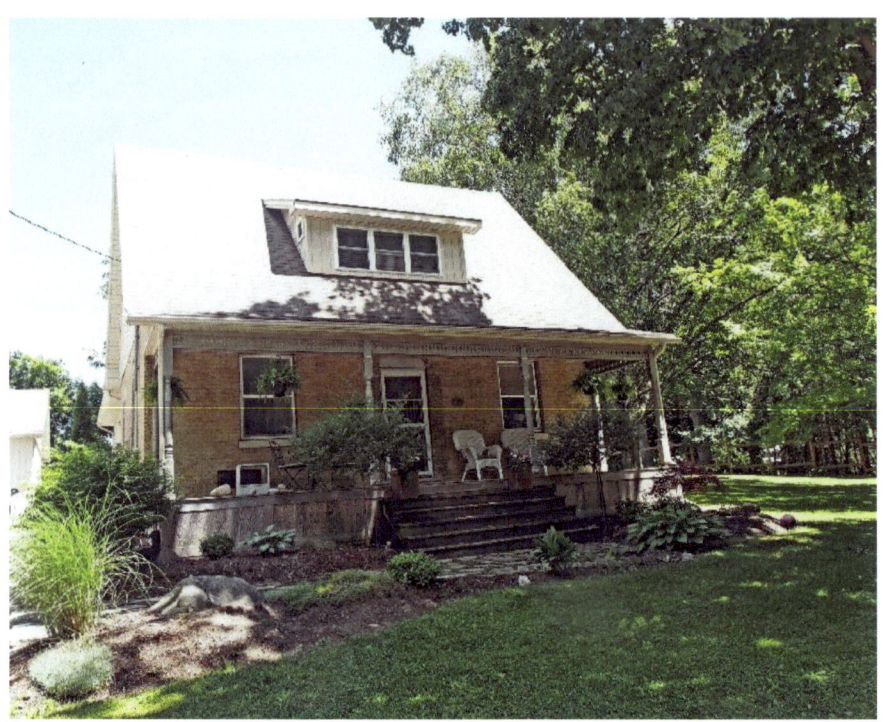

329 Oxford Street - The front section of this house was built in 1835, making it one of the oldest brick homes in Ingersoll. The solid brick walls are constructed from a locally handmade soft brick. The back brick-veneer section was added in 1890 by Bill McKay. The veranda is highlighted by the decoratively carved fascia board. The house sits on a parcel of land that was part of the original Ingersoll survey.

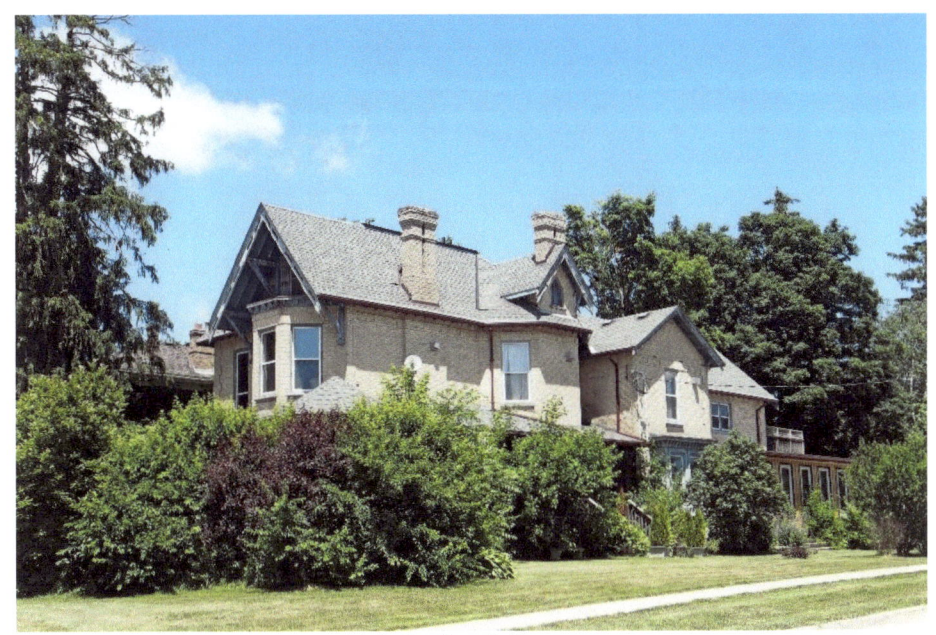

319 Oxford Street

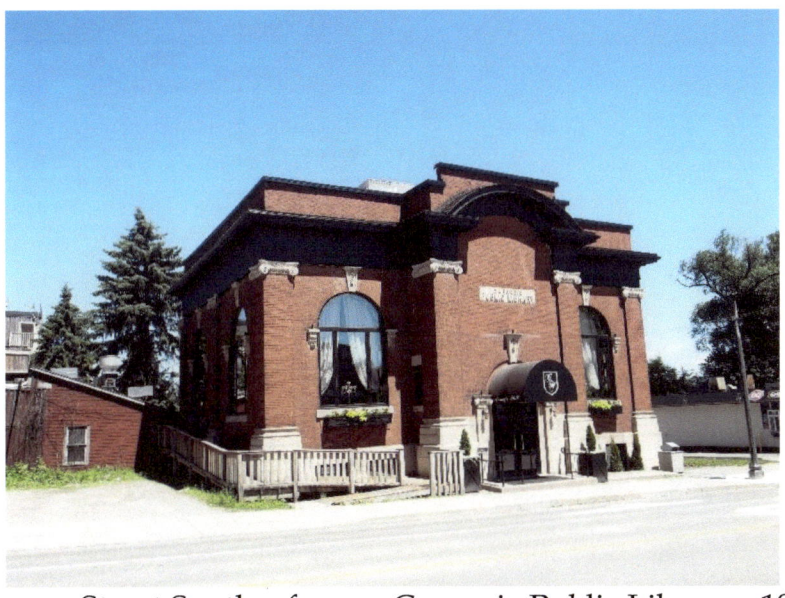

Thames Street South – former Carnegie Public Library - 1910

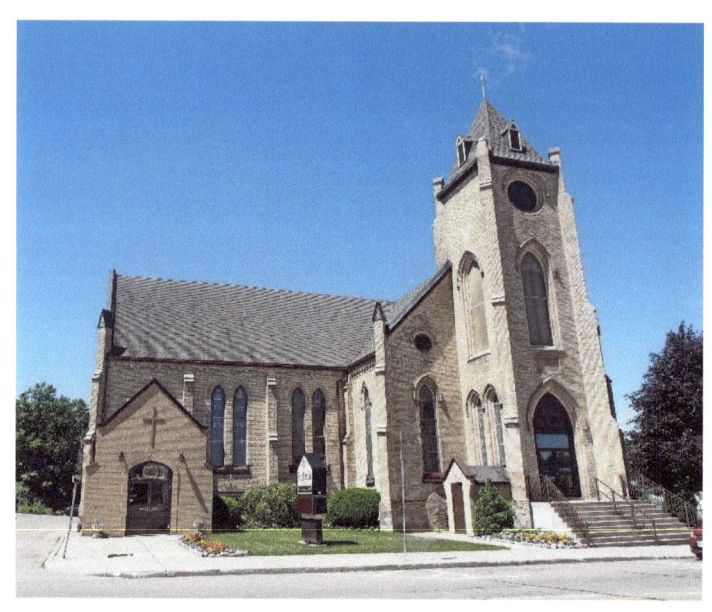

56 Thames Street South – St. Paul's Presbyterian Church – Gothic Revival – lancet windows, buttresses, three-storey tower

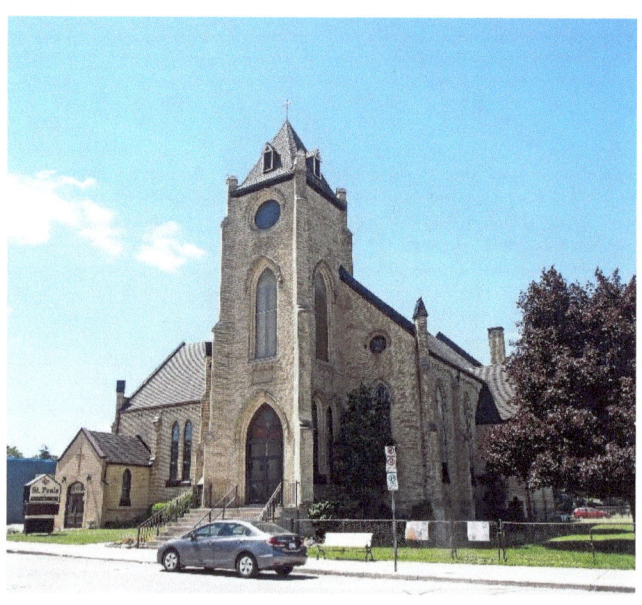

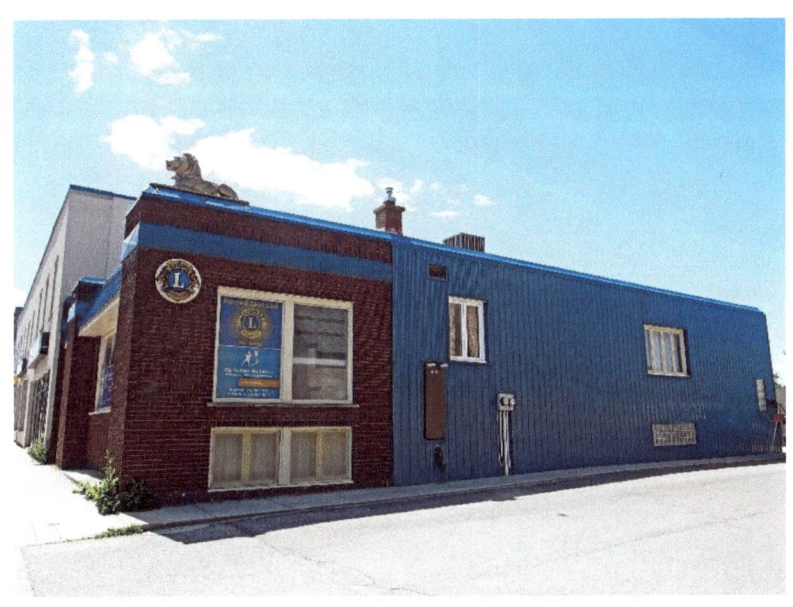

58 Thames Street South – Lions Club

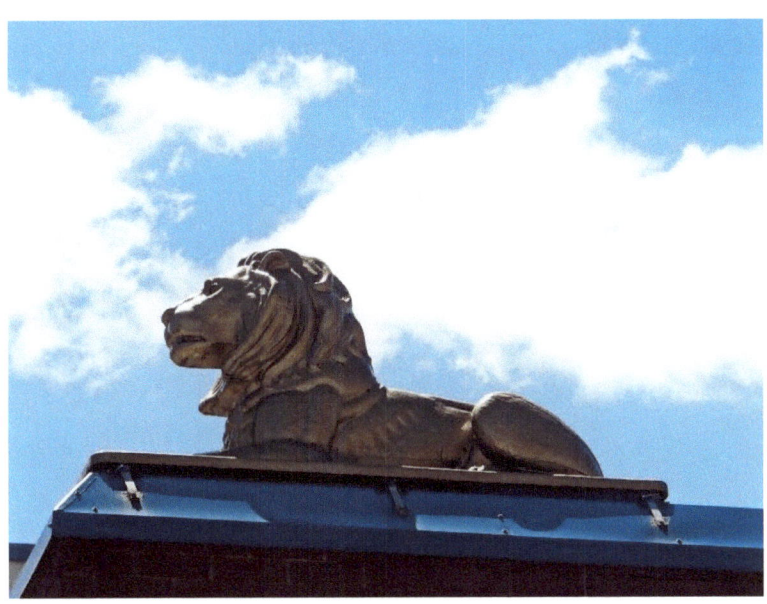

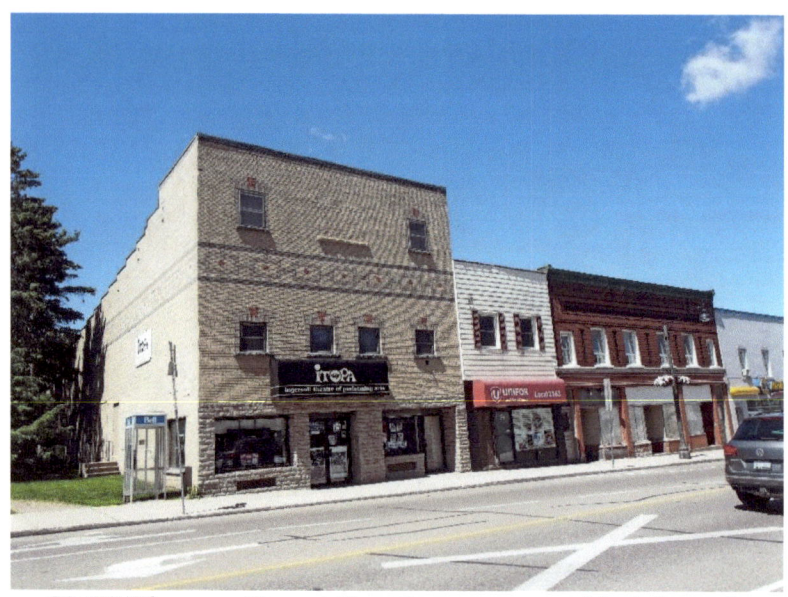

80-88 Thames Street South – patterned brickwork

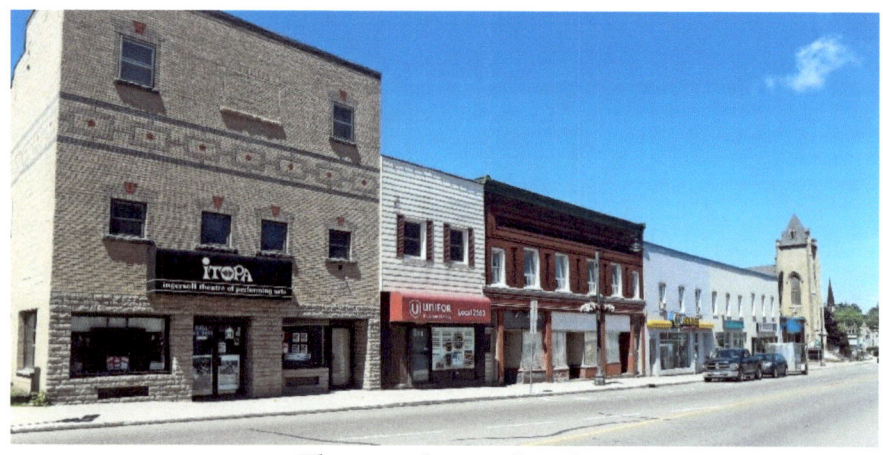

Thames Street South

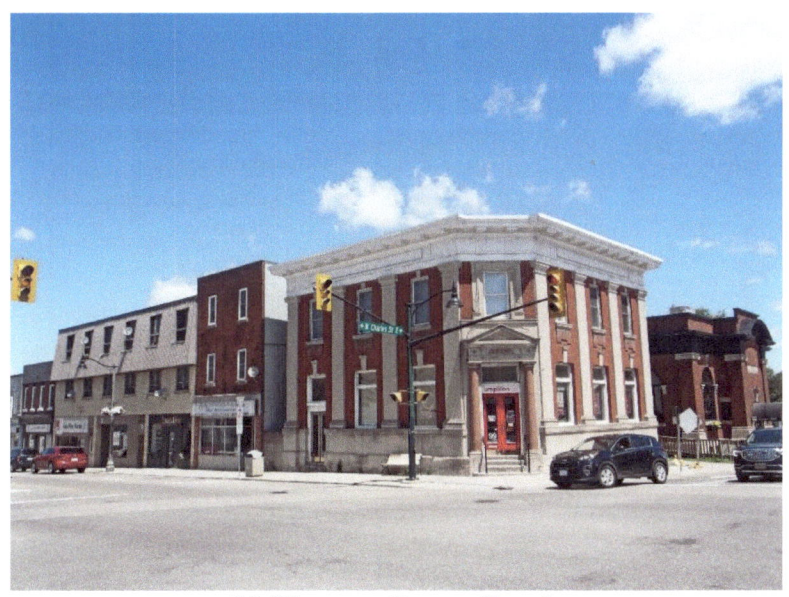

99 Thames Street South

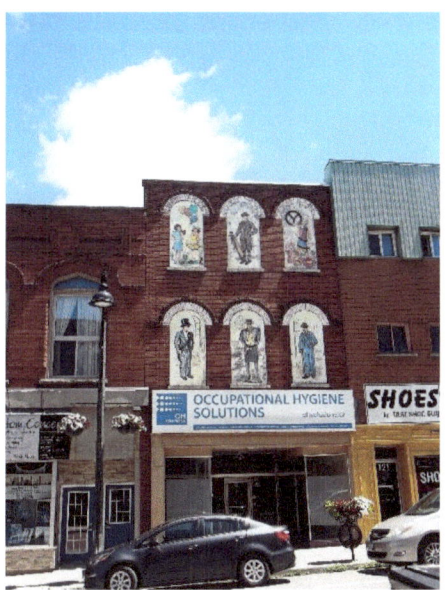

119 Thames Street South

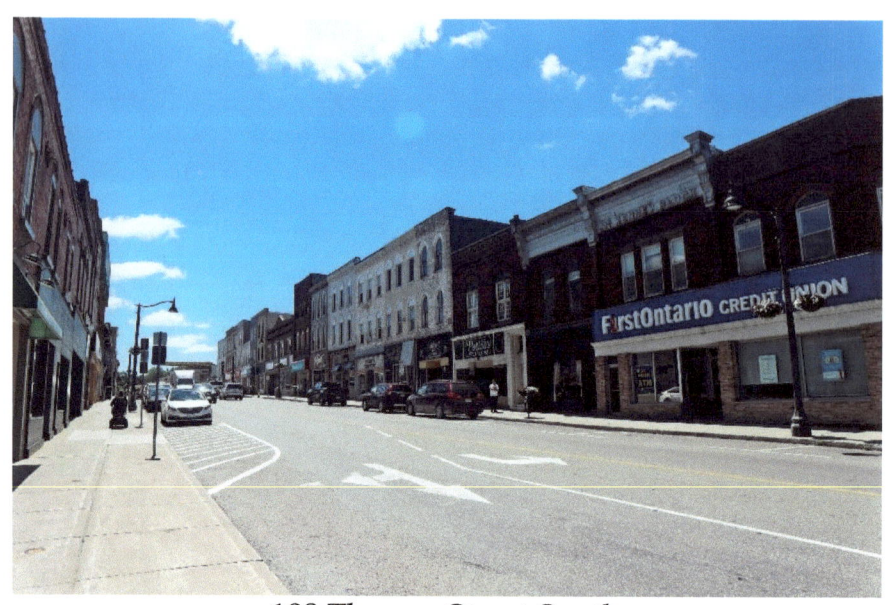
108 Thames Street South

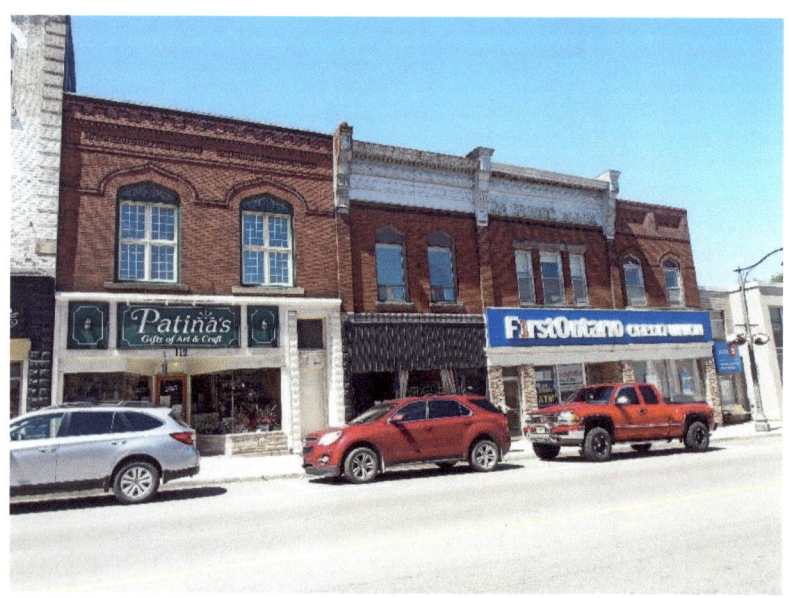
108-112 Thames Street South

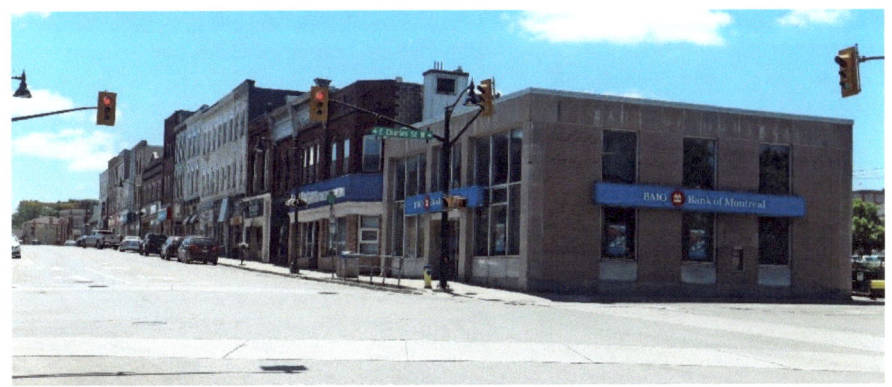

104 Thames Street South

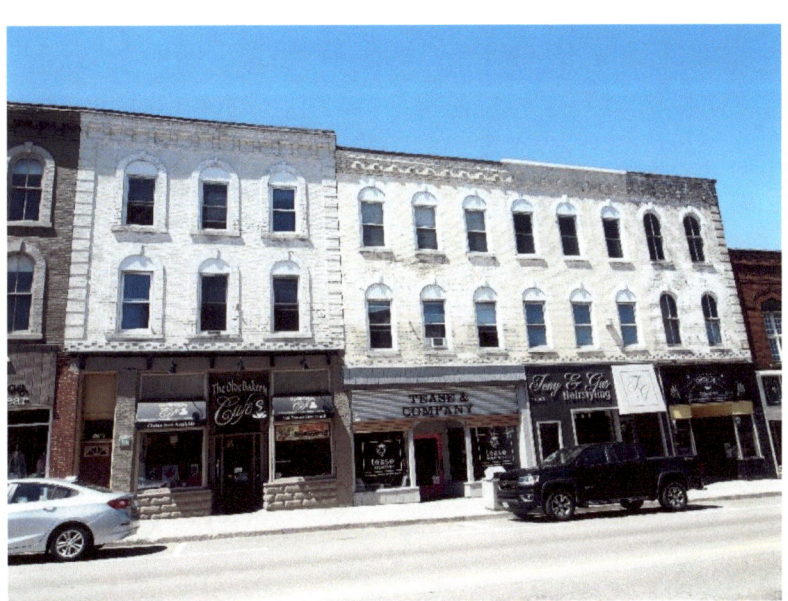

114-120 Thames Street South – voussoirs, keystones, dentil molding

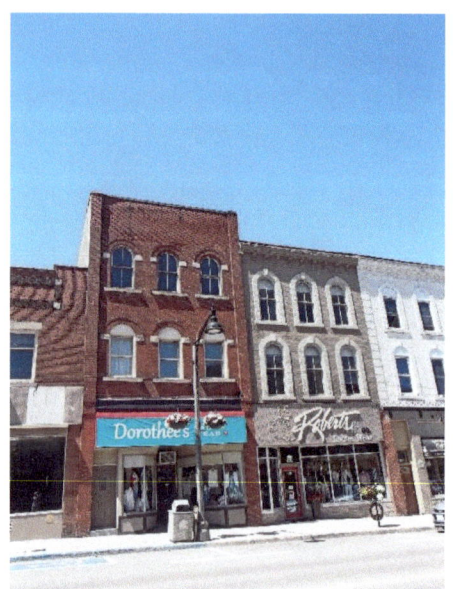

122-124 Thames Street South

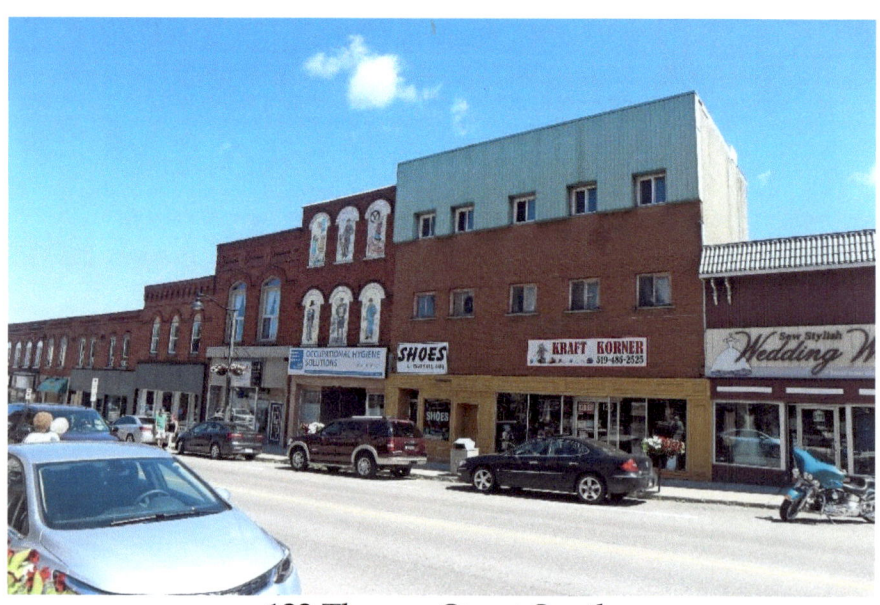

123 Thames Street South

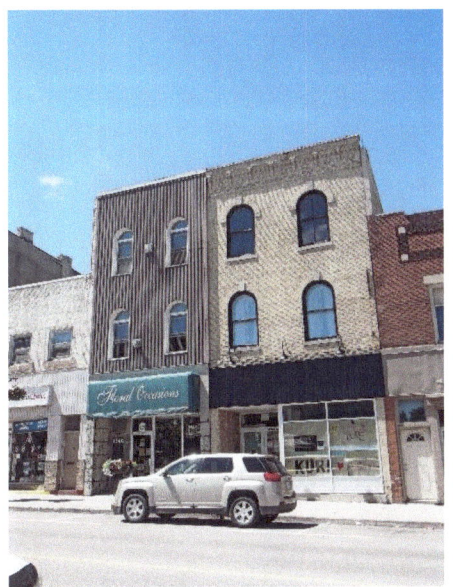

132-134 Thames Street South

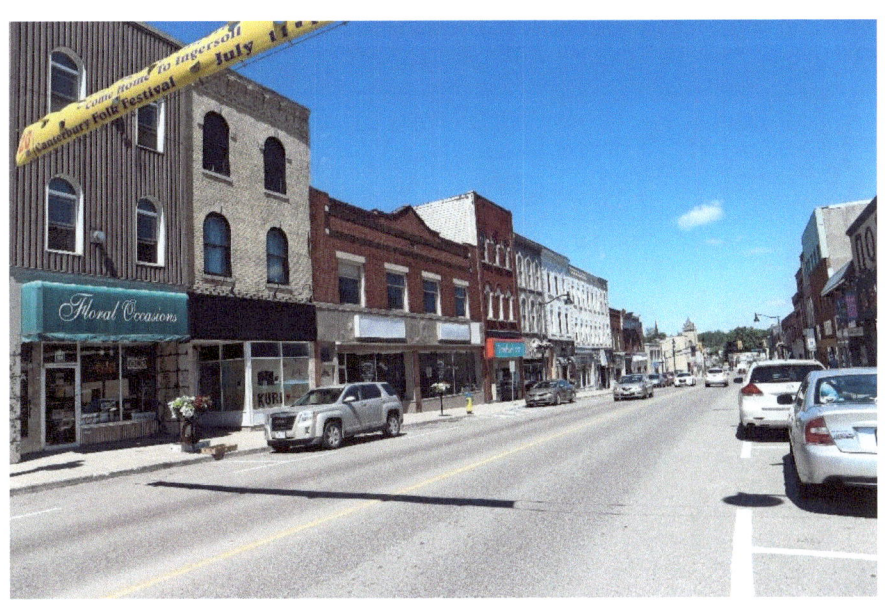

Thames Street South

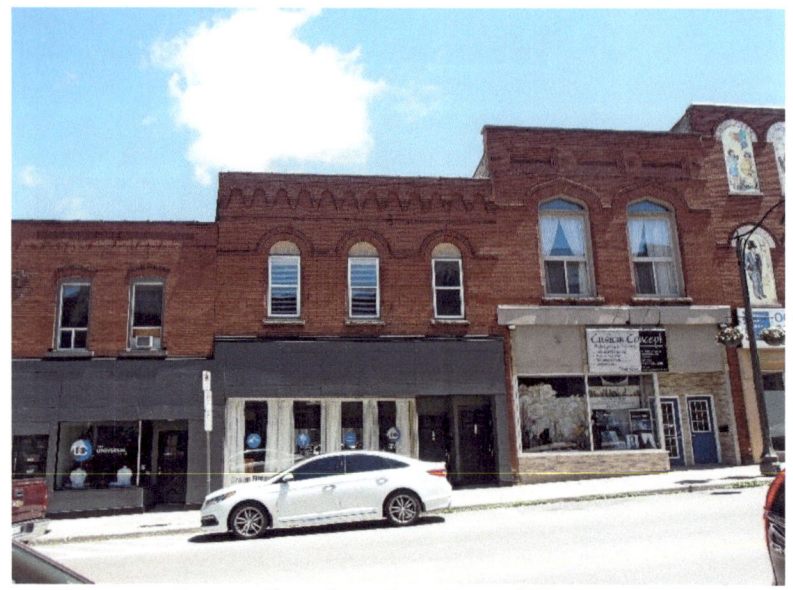

Thames Street South – dentil molding, voussoirs

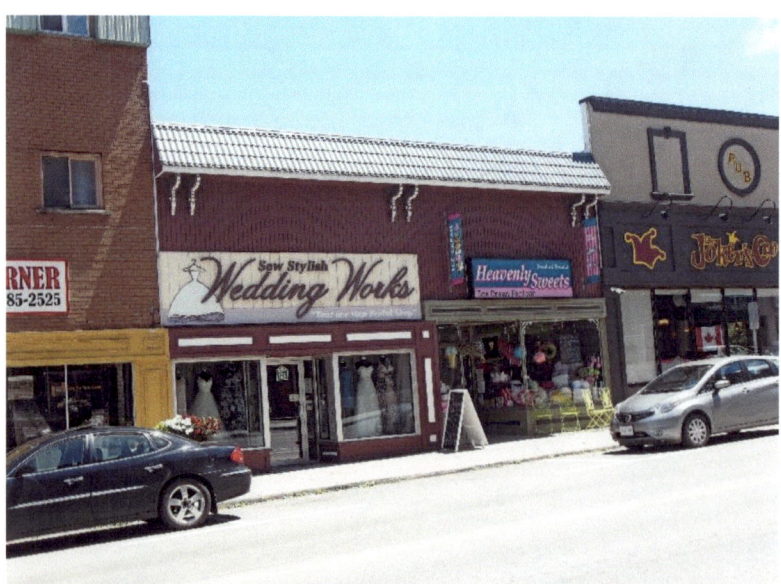

125 Thames Street South – cornice brackets

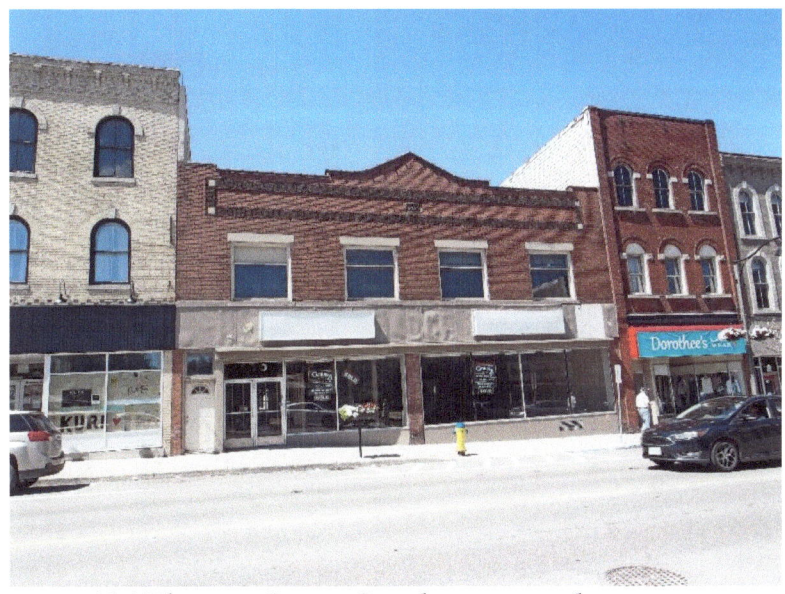

126 Thames Street South – stepped parapet

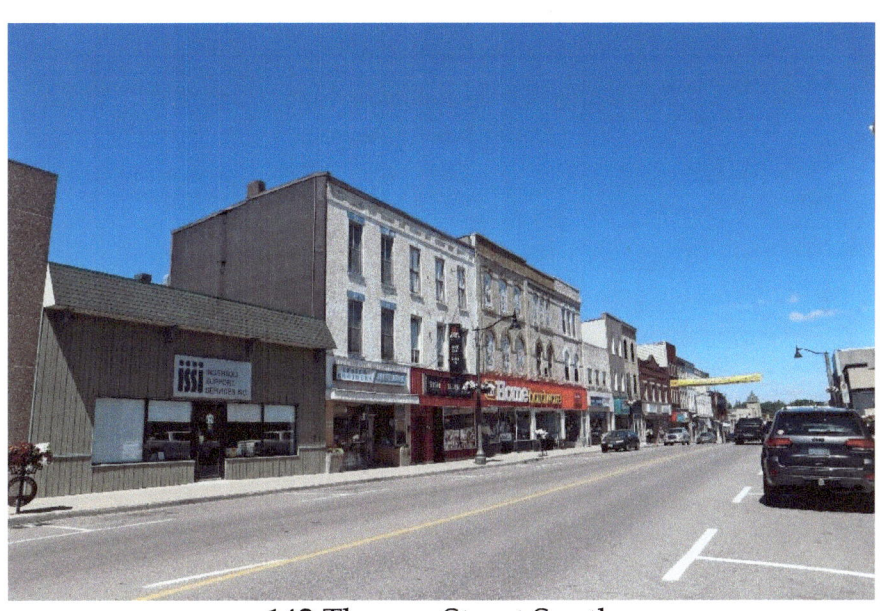

142 Thames Street South

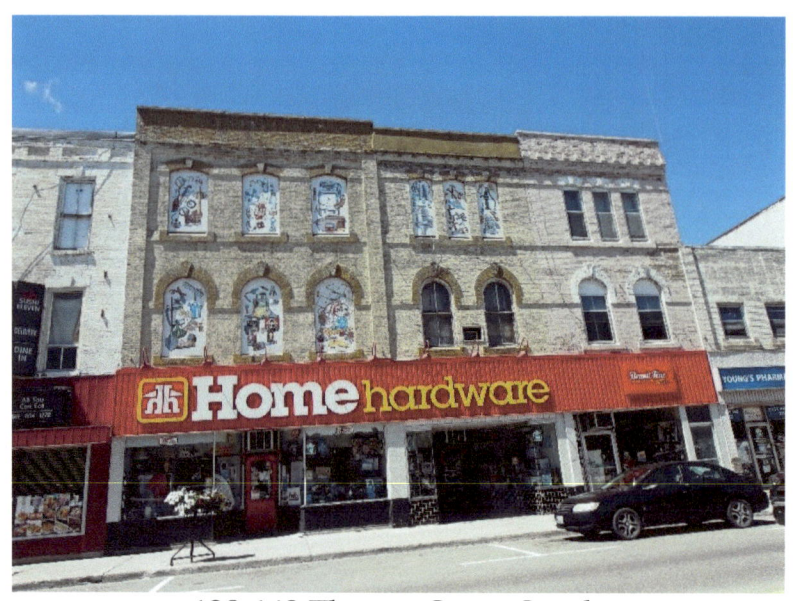
138-142 Thames Street South

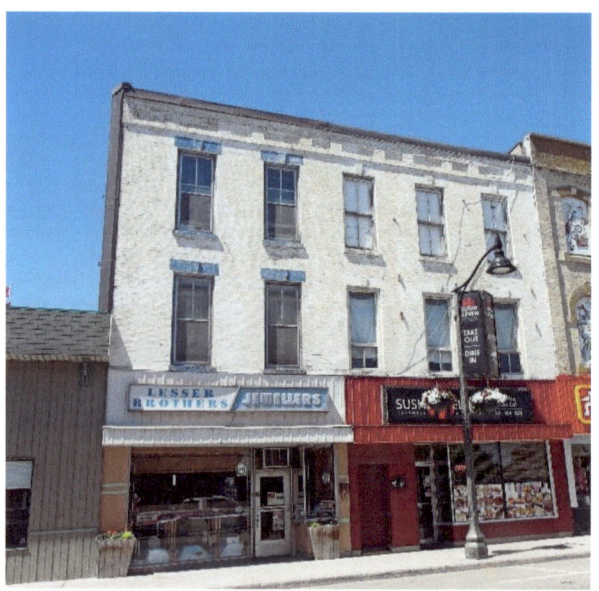
144-146 Thames Street South

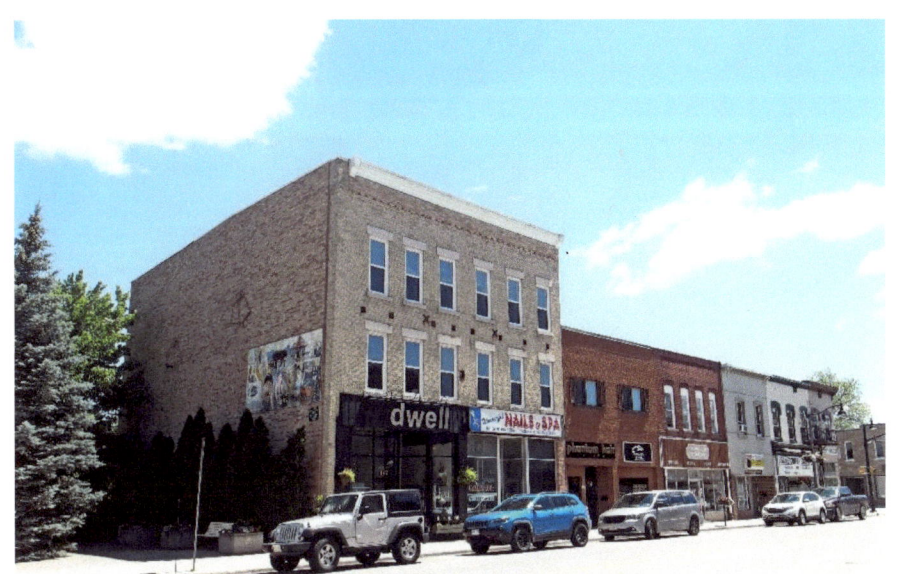

149 Thames Street South

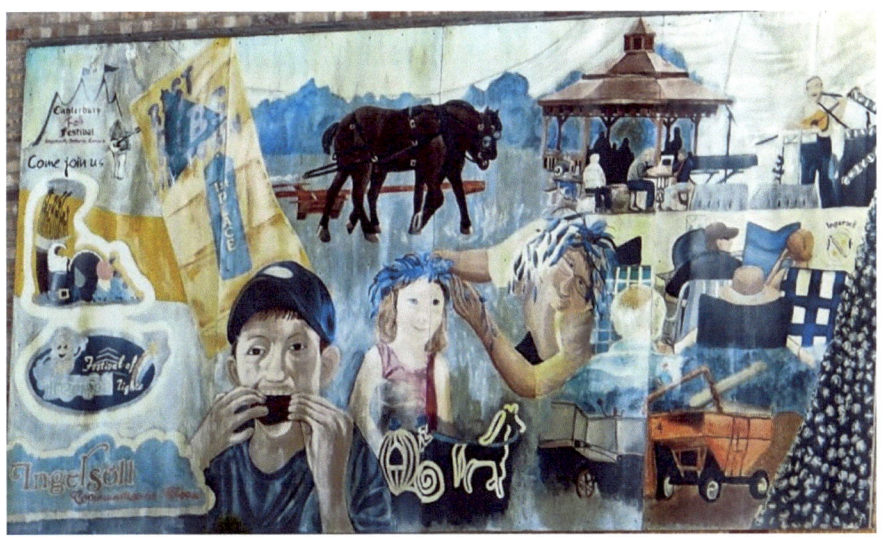

Mural

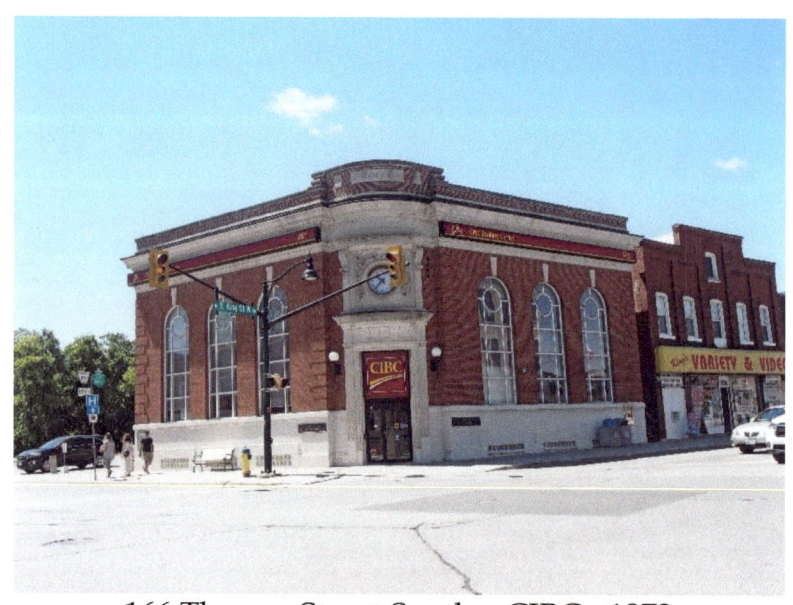

166 Thames Street South – CIBC - 1872

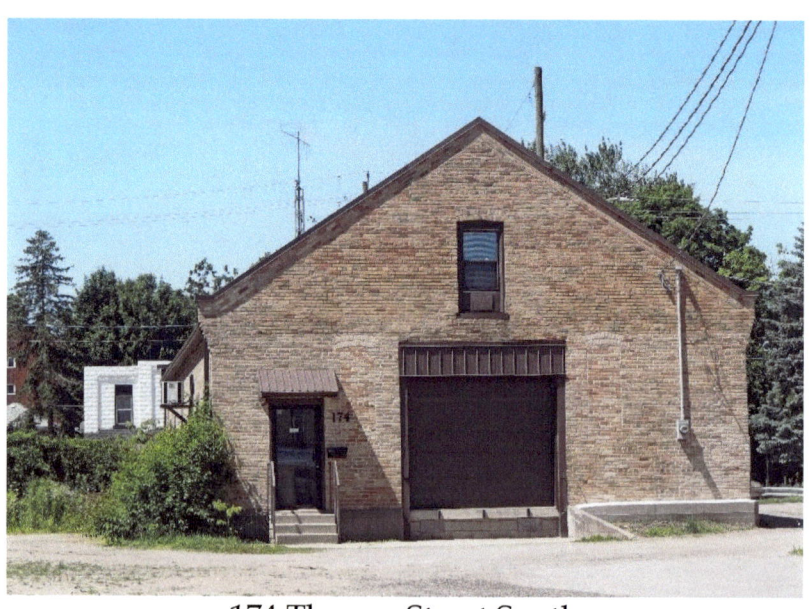

174 Thames Street South

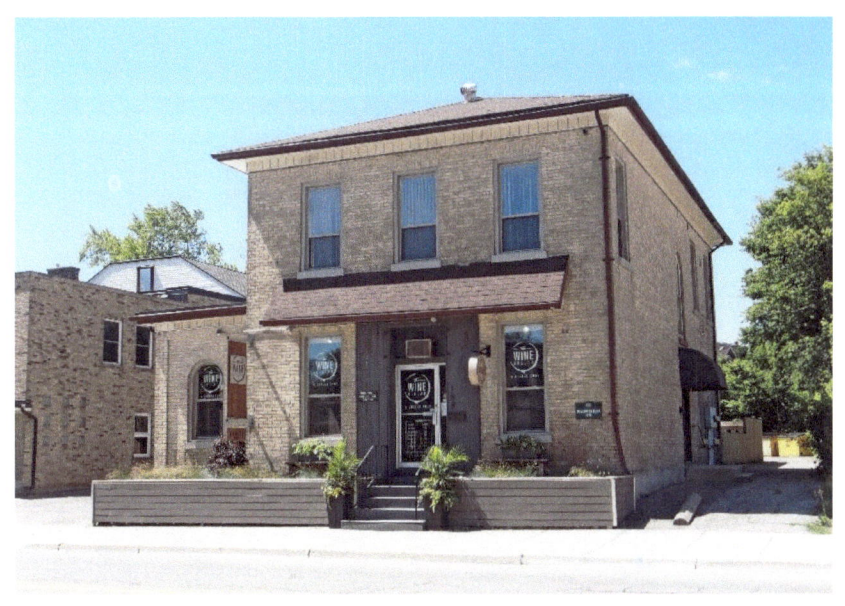

188 Thames Street South – hipped roof

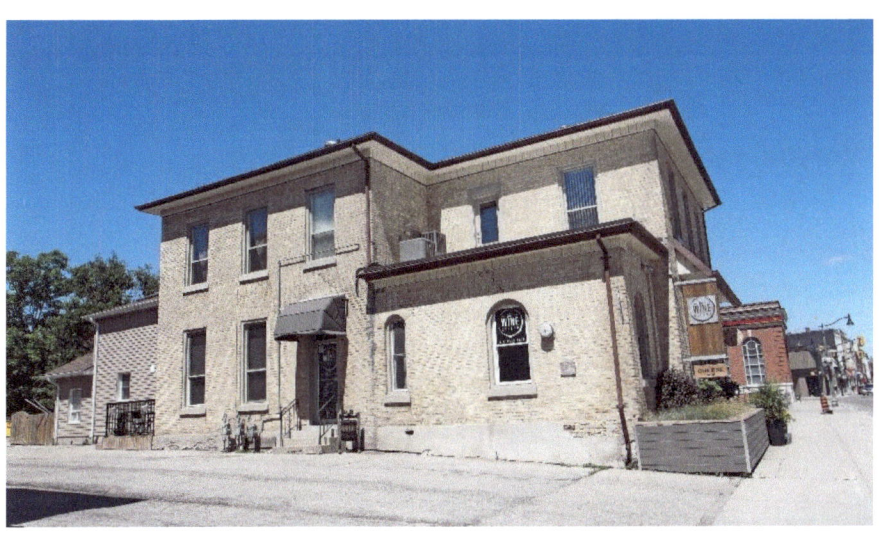

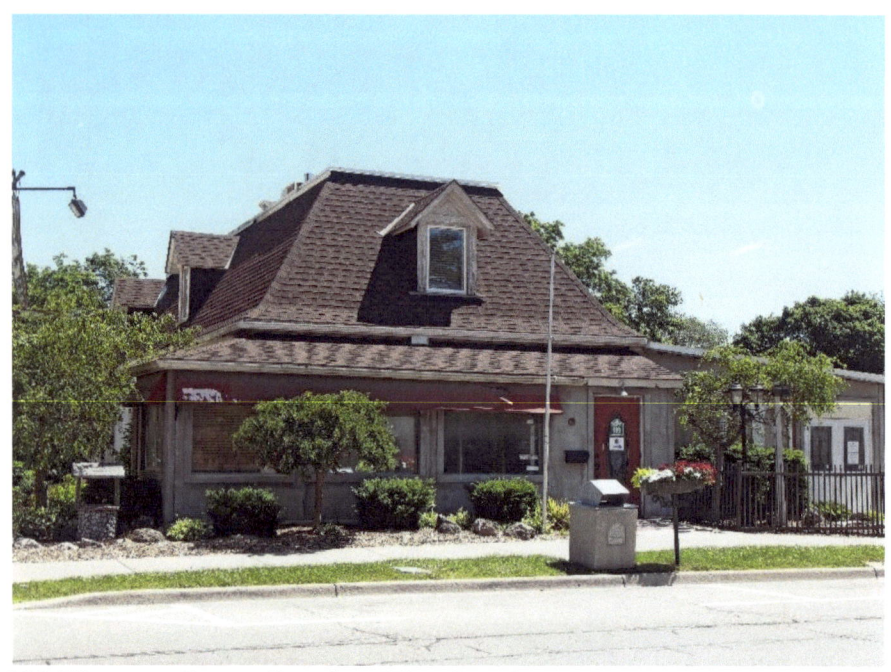

189 Thames Street South – The Smith House – James Smith emigrated from Scotland in 1862. Shortly after his arrival in Ingersoll, he married Alice Galliford, daughter of John Galliford, Ingersoll's first reeve. They moved into this house which was a small one-storey cottage at the time. As the family grew to include nine children, a wing was built on the south side which included a kitchen and a dining room. A second storey containing five bedrooms was also added. John admired the mansard roofline of the newly completed Niagara District Bank across the street and he incorporated a similar roofline in his second-storey addition. When indoor plumbing was added, one of the bedrooms was converted into a bathroom.

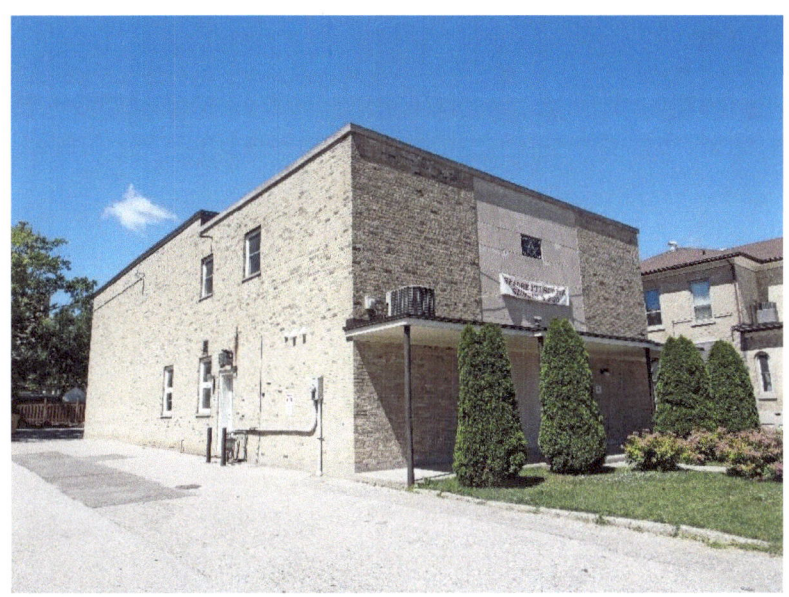

190 Thames Street South – Masonic Centre

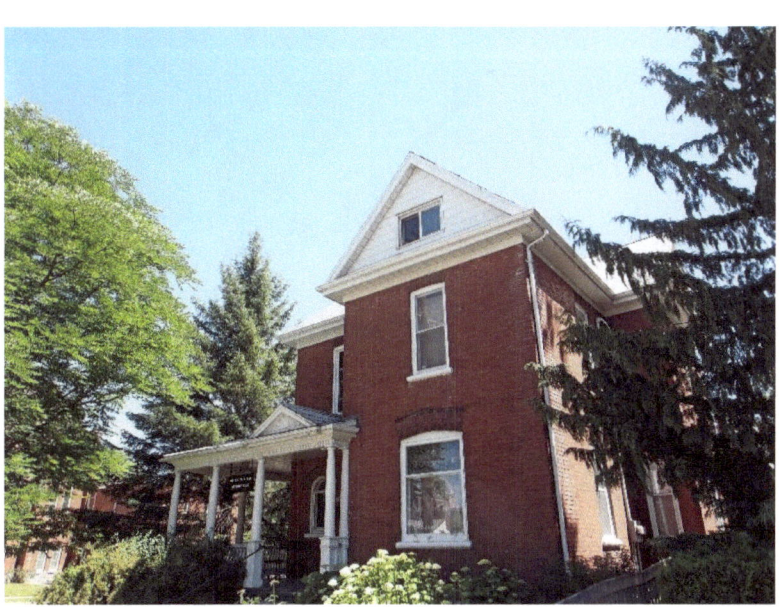

245 Thames Street South

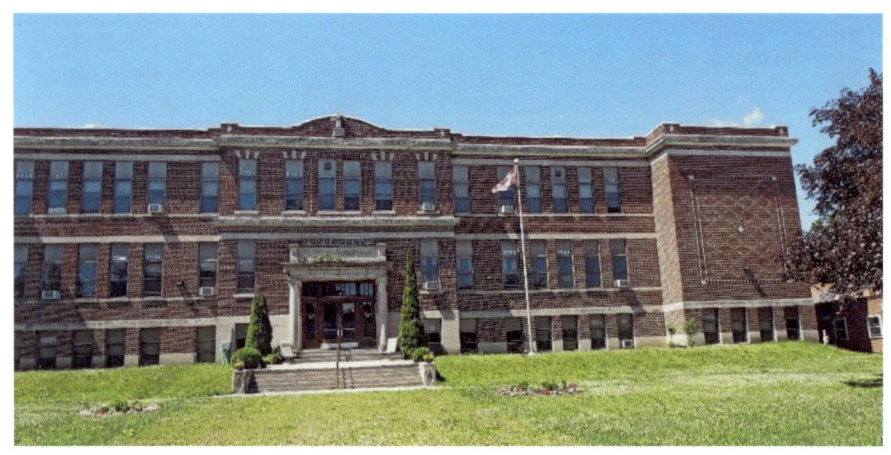

210 Thames Street South - Victory Memorial School was officially opened in September 1921. It was built as memorial to those who fought in World War I and replaced the former Central School which stood on the same grounds. Neo-Gothic (Collegiate Gothic) style – voussoirs over windows above entrance, patterned brickwork

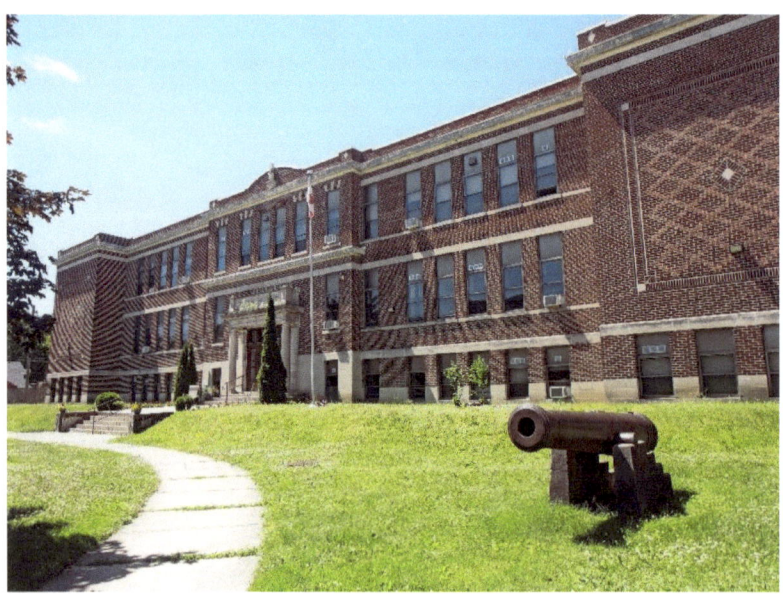

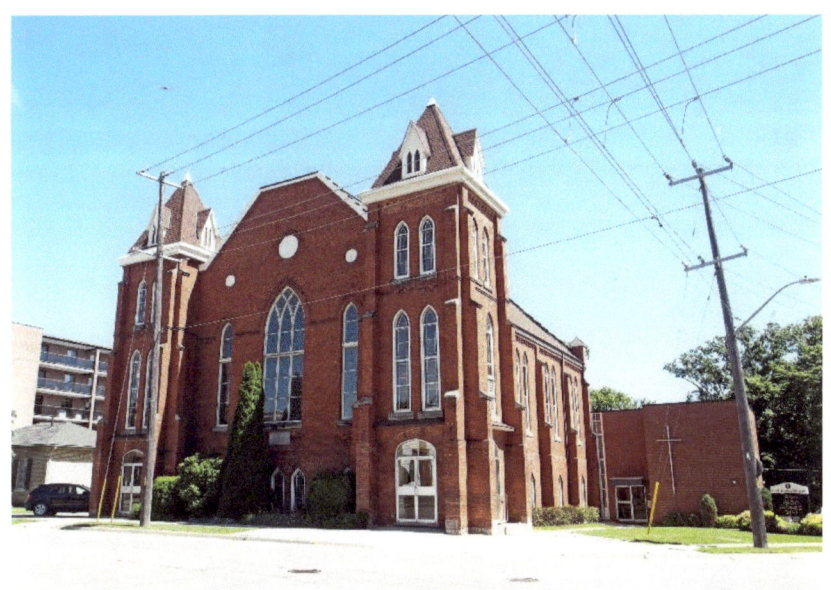

235 Thames Street South – First Baptist Church - A.D. 1890 – Gothic Revival – lancet windows, buttresses, two 3½-storey towers

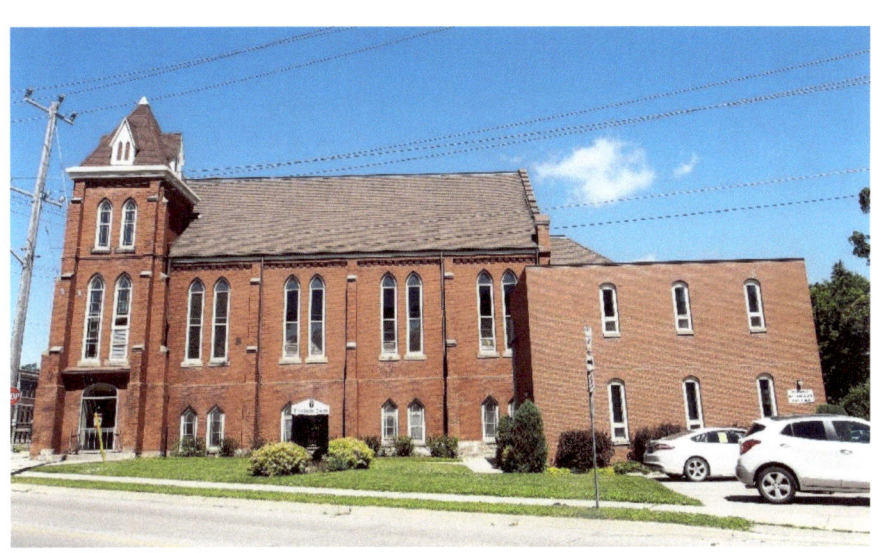

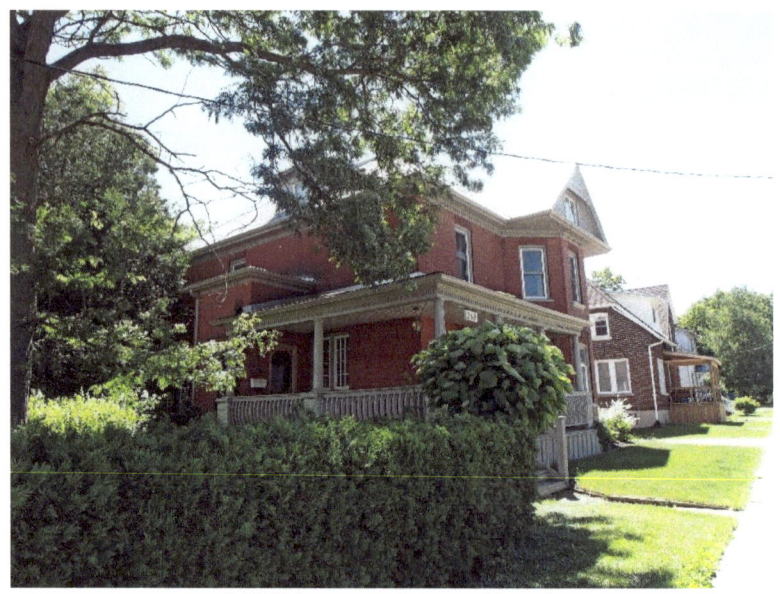
249 Thames Street South

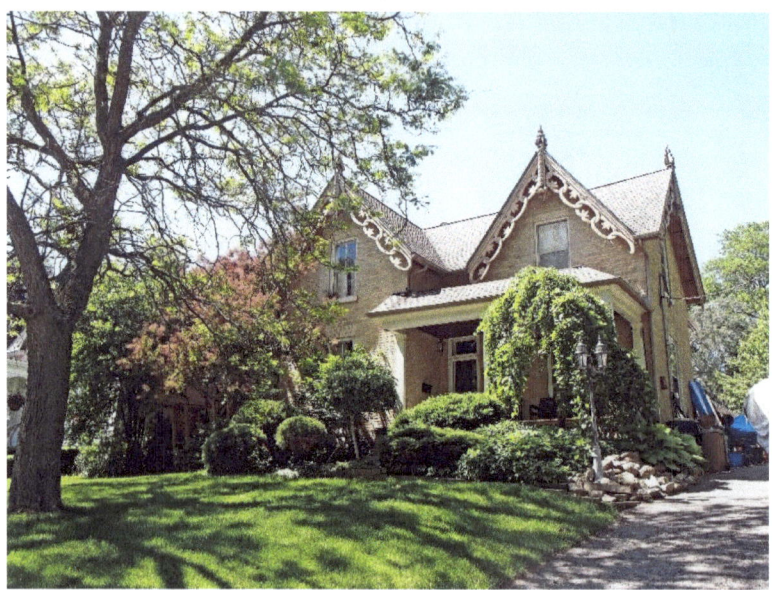
280 Thames Street South – Gothic Revival – verge board trim and finials on gables

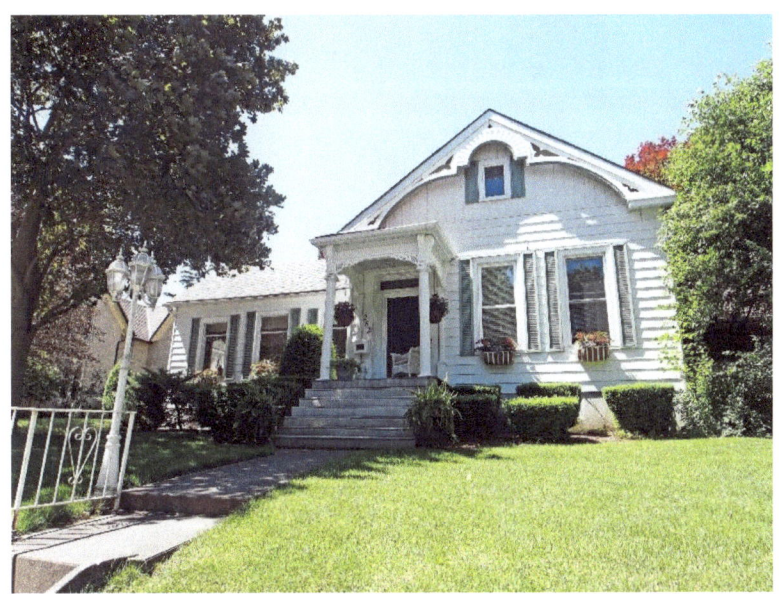

282 Thames Street South – Gothic – verge board trim

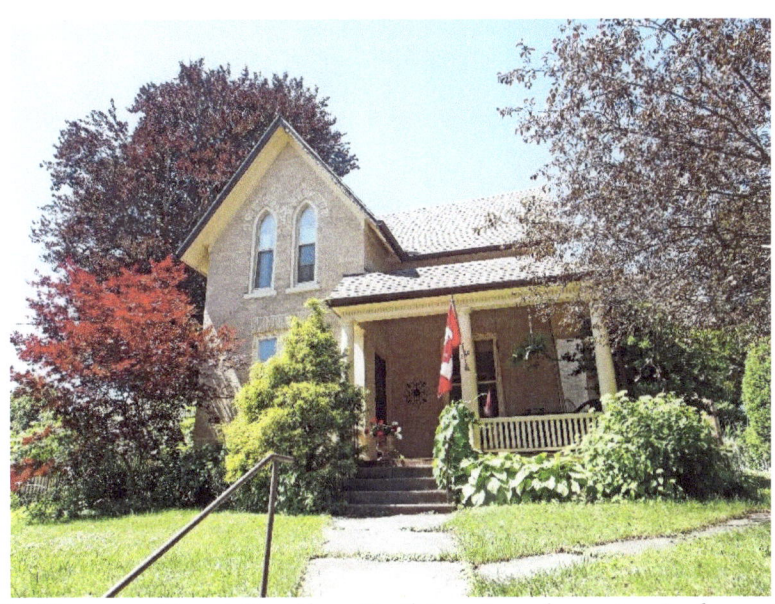

286 Thames Street South – Gothic – two lancet windows in gable

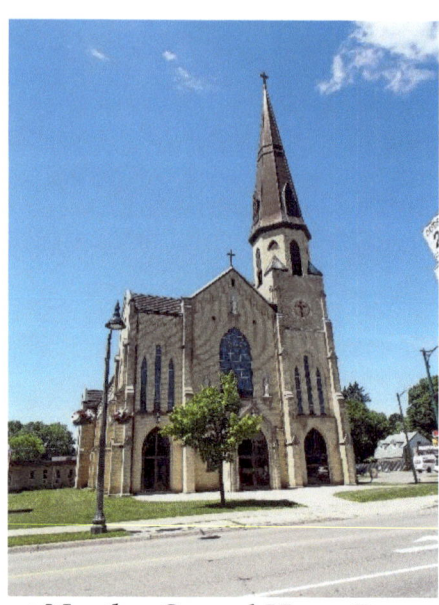

131 Thames Street North – Sacred Heart Roman Catholic Church – c. 1875-1879 – Gothic Revival – lancet windows, buttresses, tower with steeple

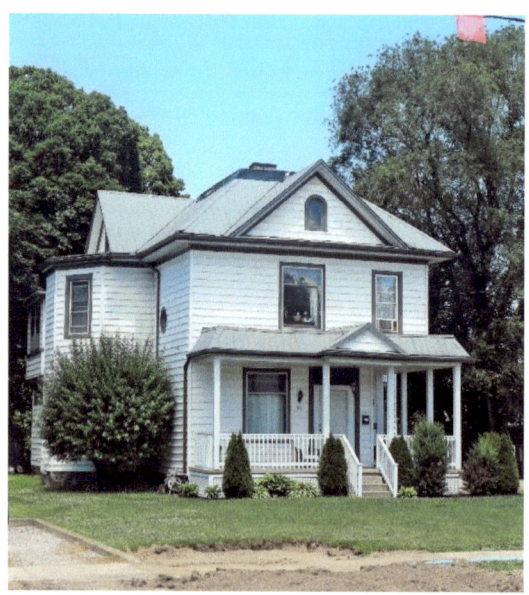

96 Charles Street West

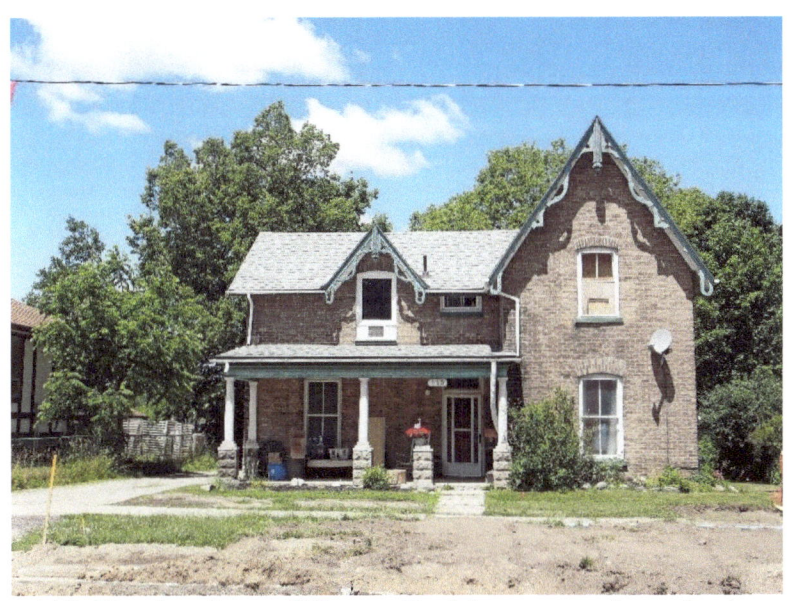

110 Charles Street West – Gothic – verge board trim

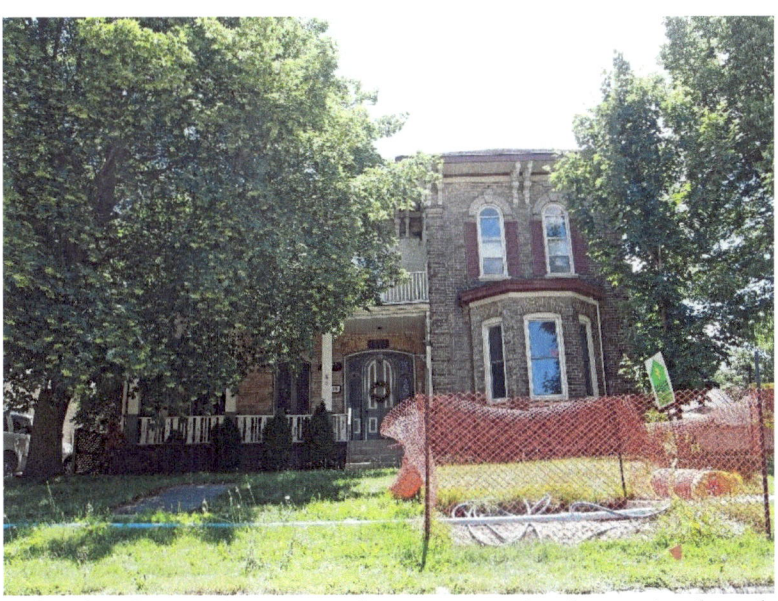

111 Charles Street West – Italianate – paired cornice brackets, bay window

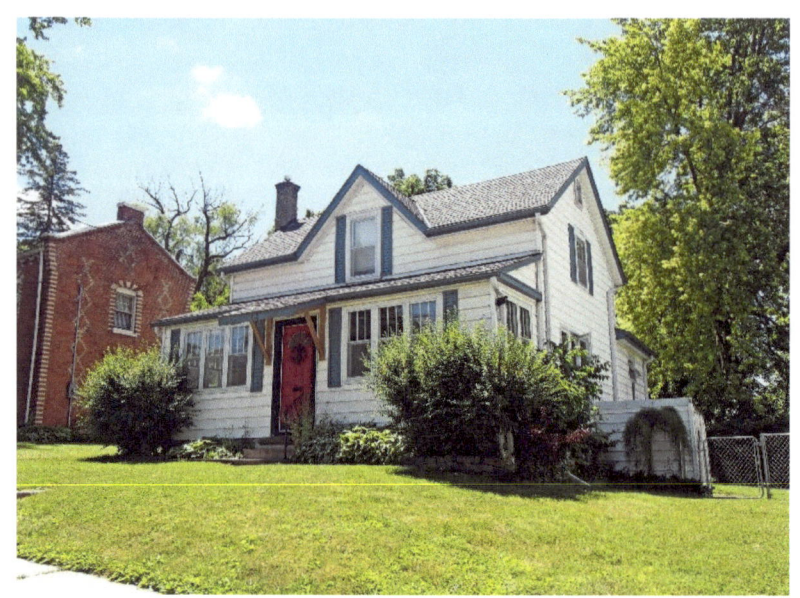
112 Charles Street West

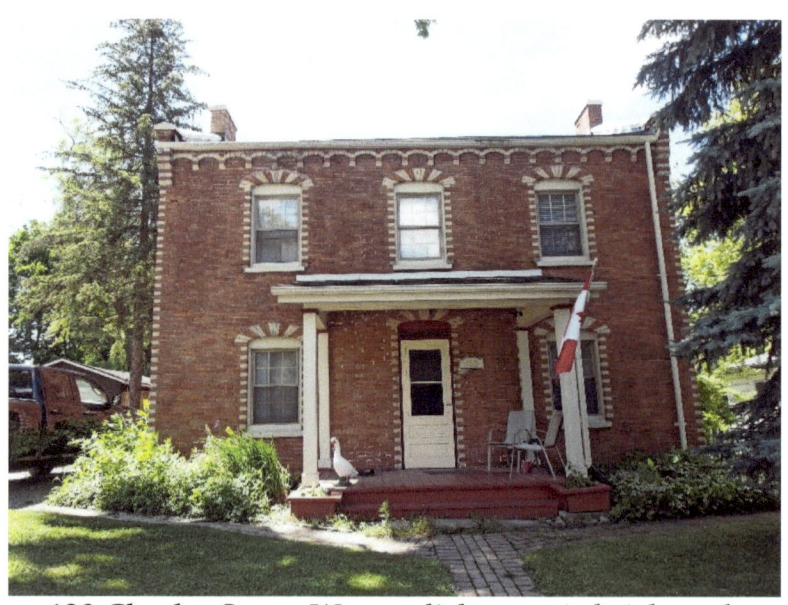
120 Charles Street West – dichromatic brickwork

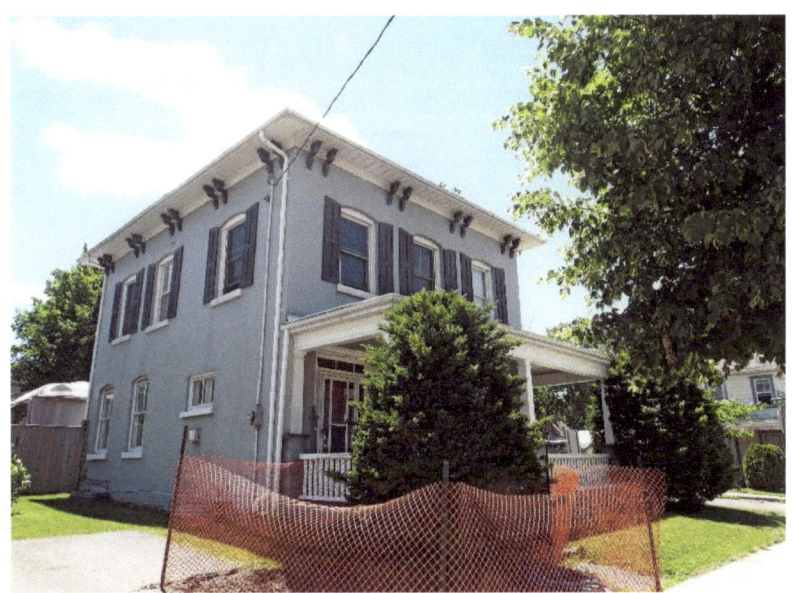
123 Charles Street West – paired cornice brackets

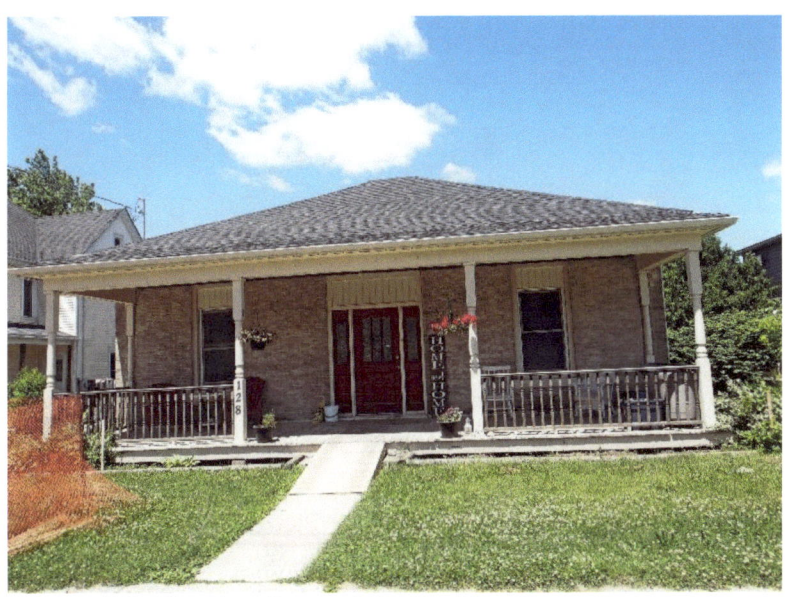
128 Charles Street West – Regency Cottage

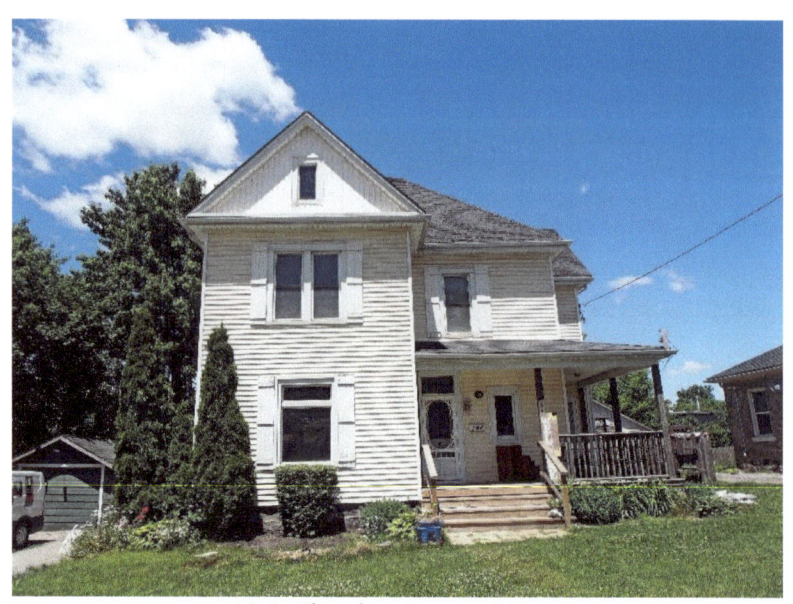
136 Charles Street West

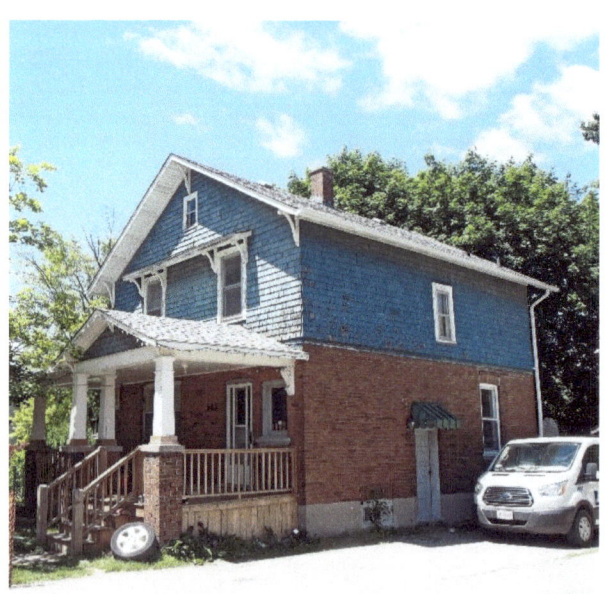
142 Charles Street West

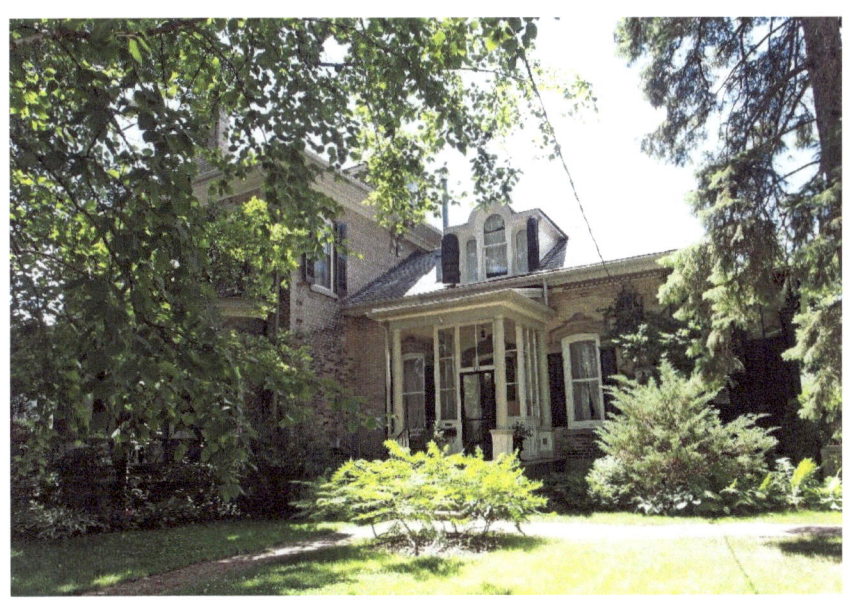

138 Charles Street West – three-window dormer above entrance

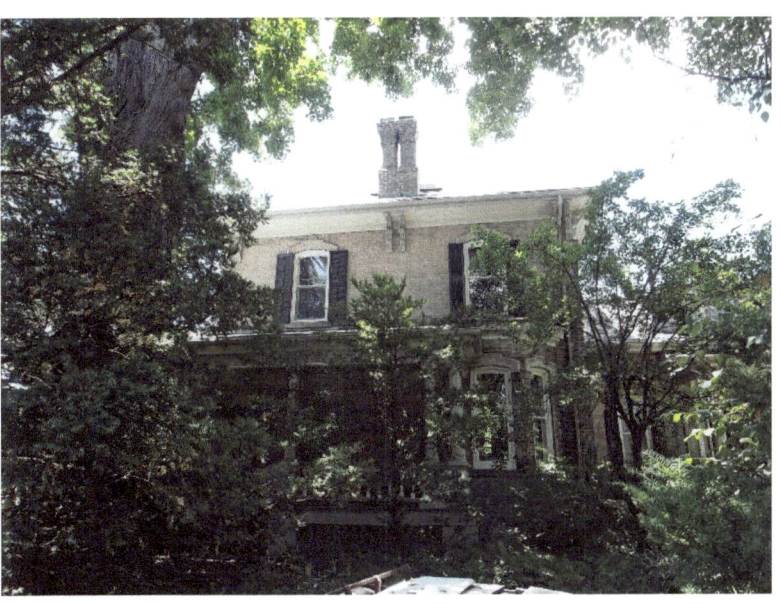

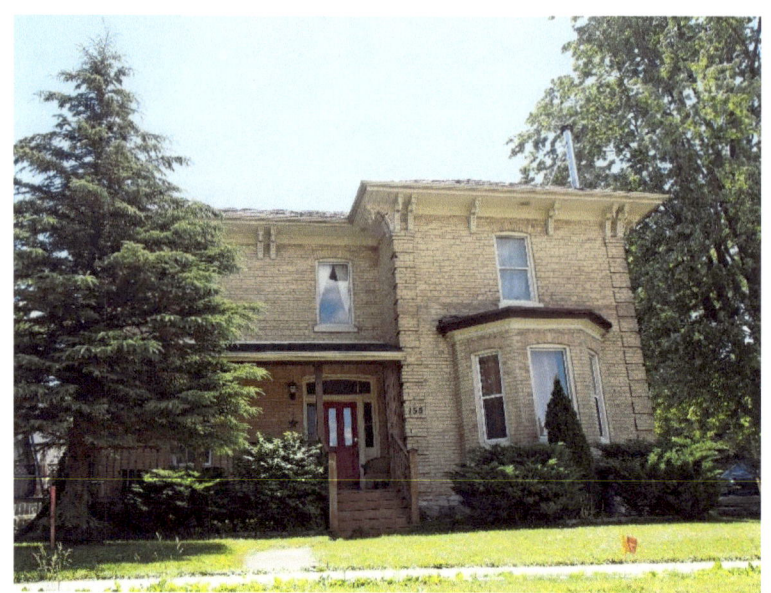

155 Charles Street West – paired cornice brackets, corner quoins, bay window

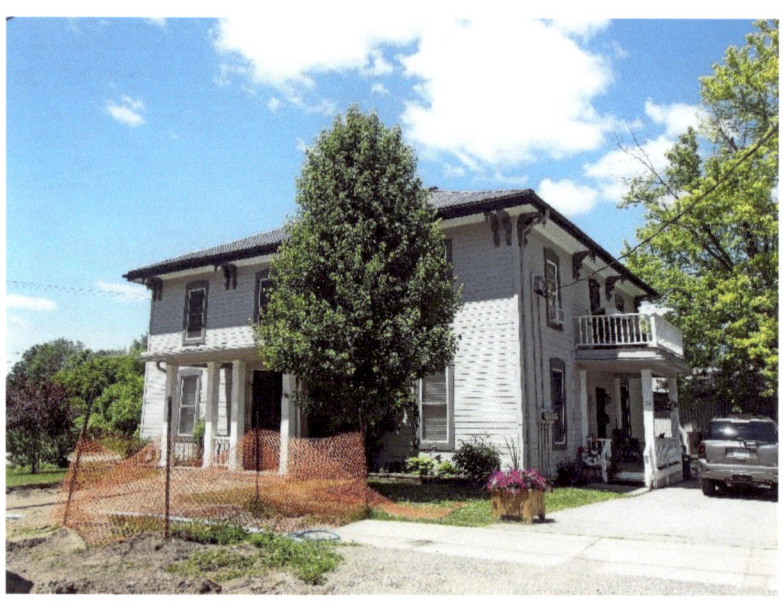

156 Charles Street West – paired cornice brackets

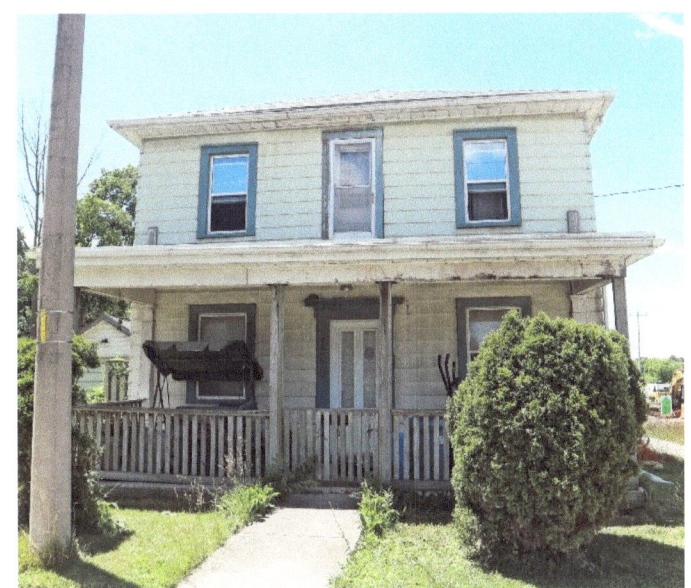

100 Albert Street – two storeys

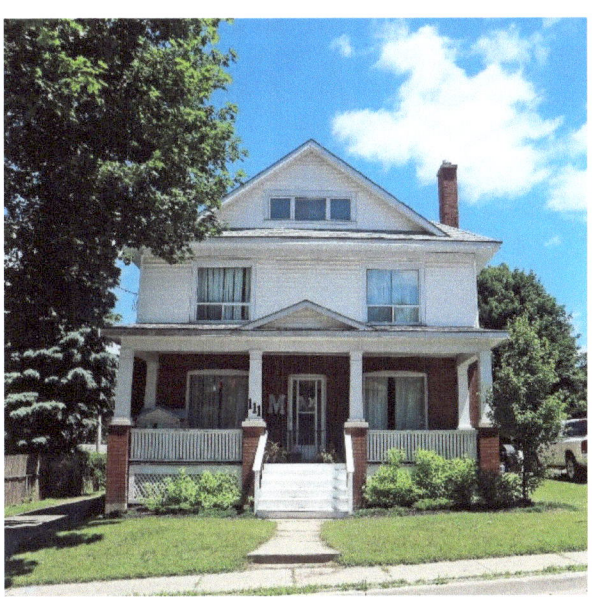

111 Albert Street - Edwardian

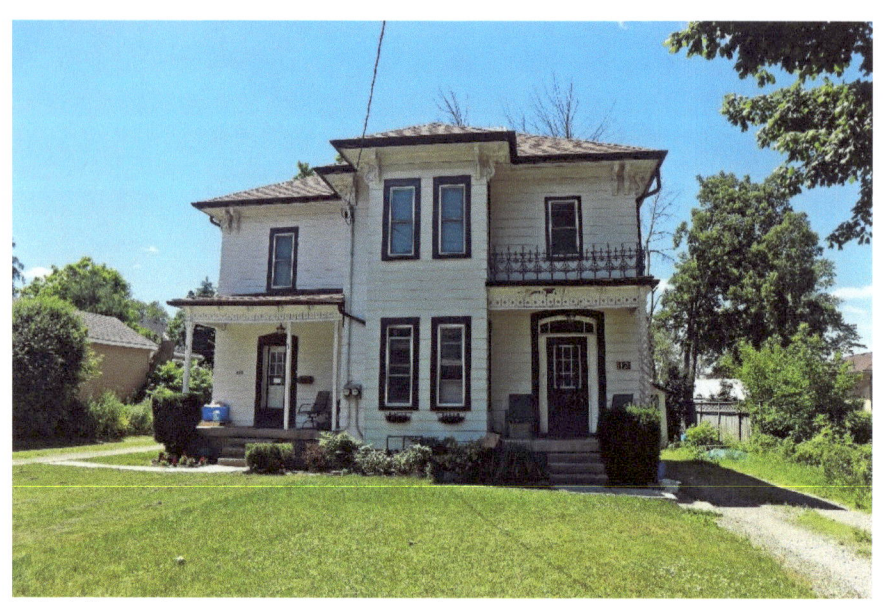

112 Albert Street – two-storey frontispiece, iron cresting above entrance door

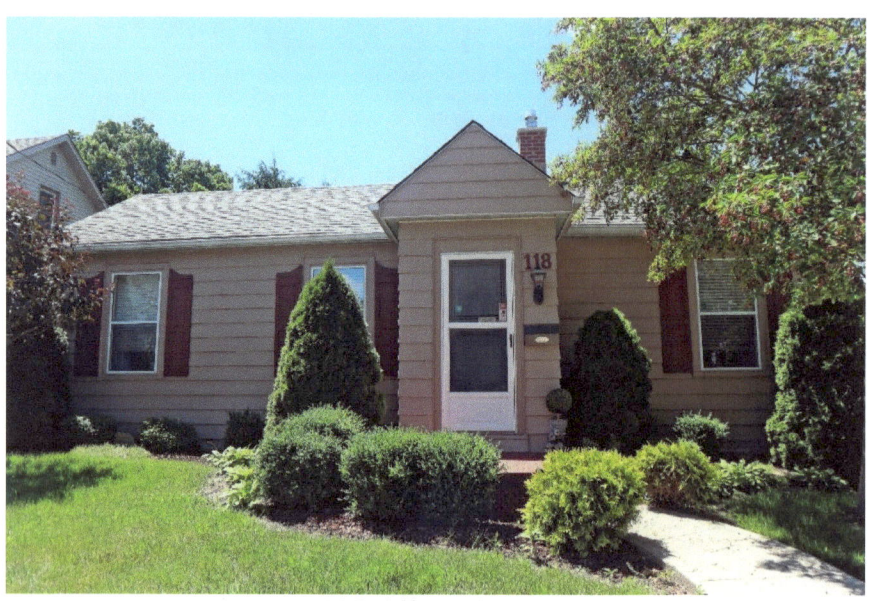

118 Albert Street

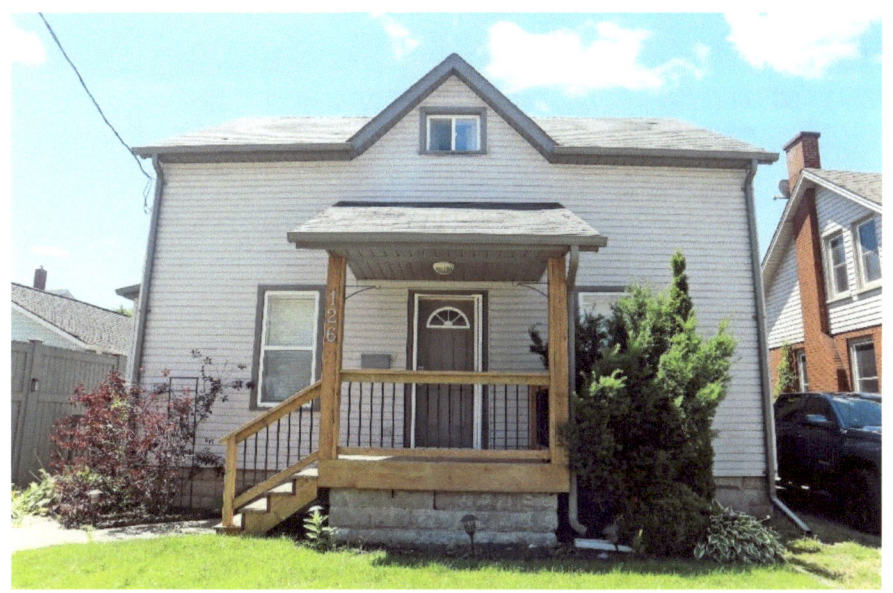

126 Albert Street

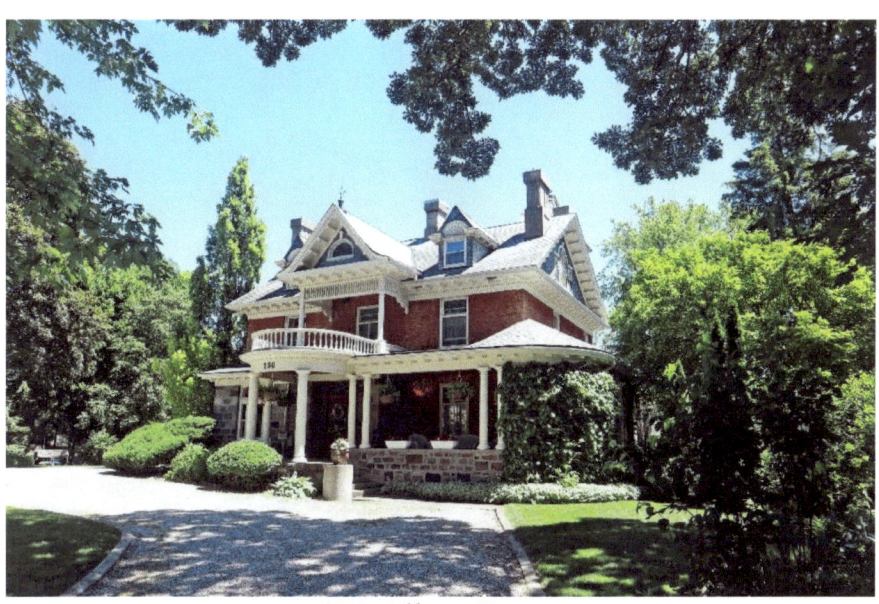

250 Albert Street

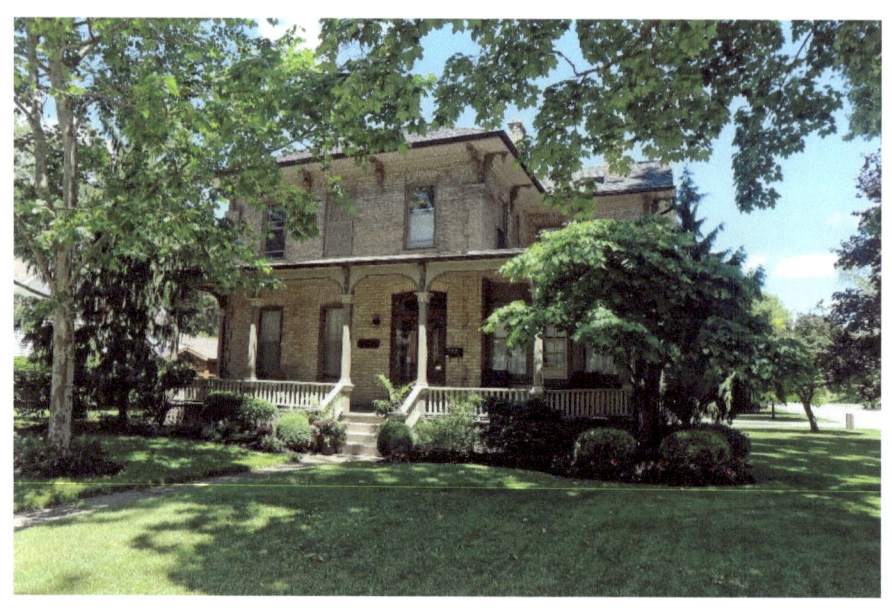

235 Albert Street – cornice brackets

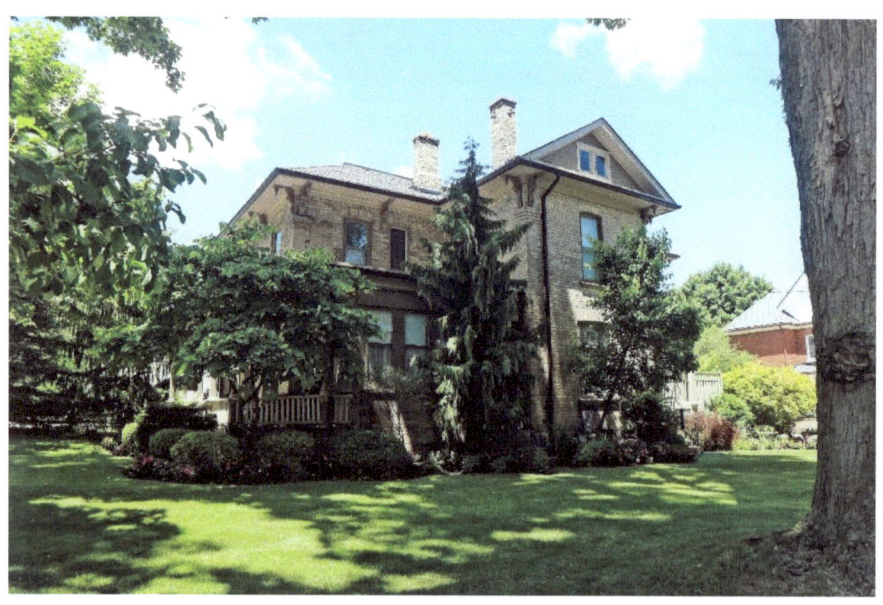

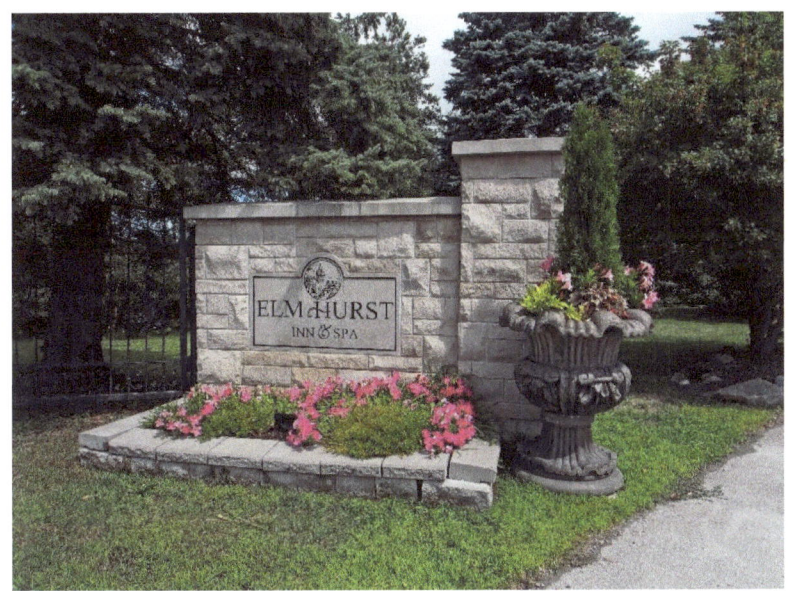

415 Harris Street – Elm Hurst Inn & Spa – 1872

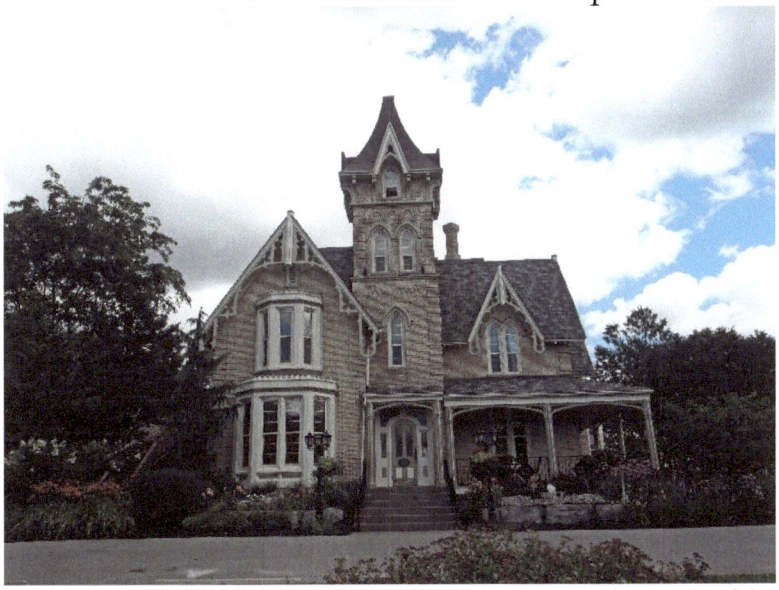

Sidelights and transom windows surrounding double entrance doors, bay window, oriel window

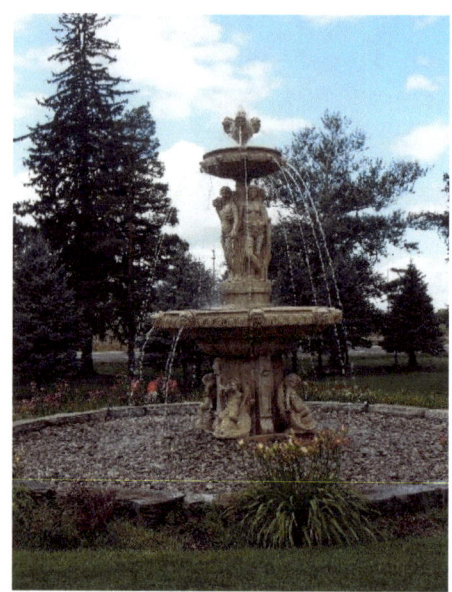

Fountain

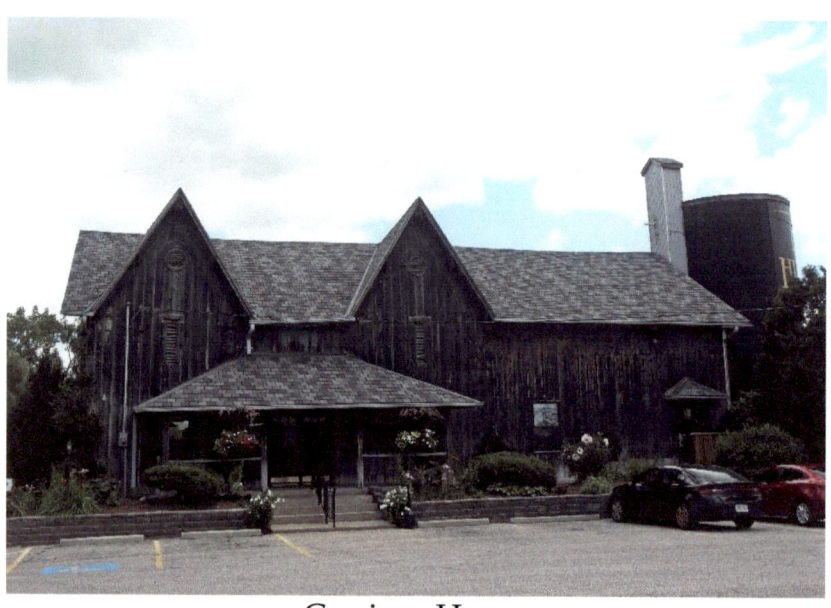

Carriage House

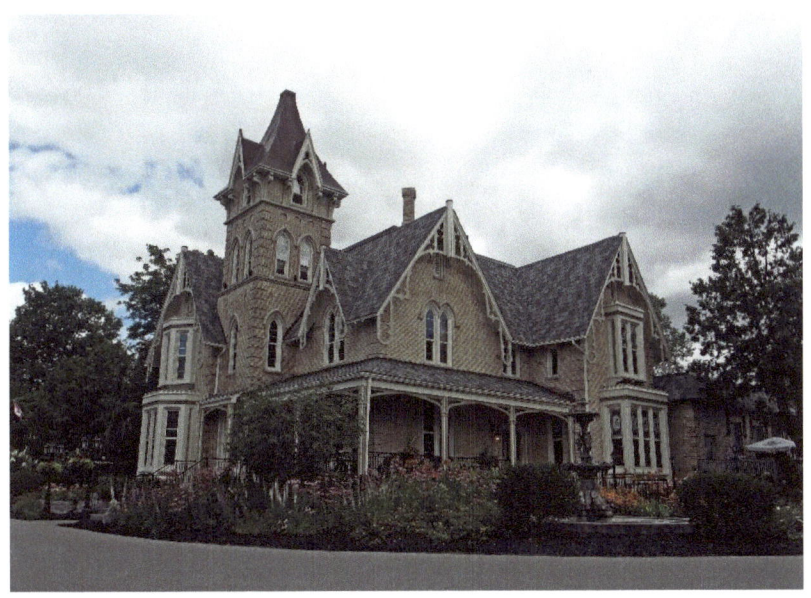

3½-storey tower with corner quoins, drip molds over Gothic style windows, decorative brickwork, elaborate verge board trim on gables, bay windows, wraparound veranda

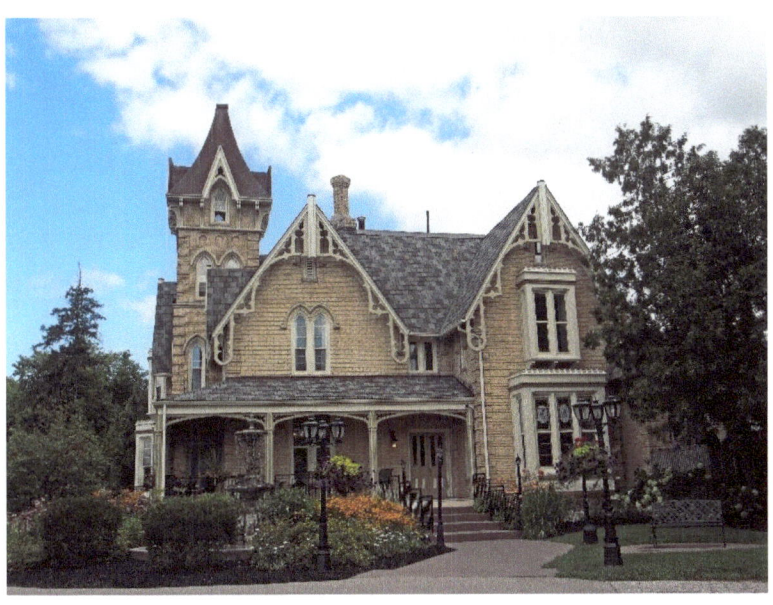

Other Books by Barbara Raue

Coins of Gold
Arrows, Indians and Love
The Life and Times of Barbara
The Cromwell Family Book
Laura Secord Discovered
Daddy Where Are You?

Montana Series
Book 1: Montana Dream
Book 2: Life on the Montana Frontier
Book 3: Montana to Boston and Back
Book 4: Montana Sons Go to War
Book 5: Montana Sons Return from War

© 2019 by Barbara Raue - All the photos in this book have been taken with my cameras. I own the rights to them.

www.ingramcontent.com/pod-product-compliance
Lightning Source LLC
Chambersburg PA
CBHW040234220526
45473CB00001B/235